Teaching Parents to Do Projects at Home

A TOOL KIT FOR PARENT EDUCATORS

Teaching Parents to Do Projects at Home

A TOOL KIT FOR PARENT EDUCATORS

Judy Harris Helm
Stacy Berg
Pam Scranton
Rebecca Wilson

TEACHERS
COLLEGE
PRESS

Teachers College, Columbia University
New York and London

Published by Teachers College Press, 1234 Amsterdam Avenue, New York, NY 10027

ISBN 0-8077-4550-2 (paper)

Printed on acid-free paper
Manufactured in the United States of America

12   11   10   09   08   07   06   05   8   7   6   5   4   3   2   1

Contents

The Family Project Planning Journal

El Diario de los Proyectos para la Familia

Acknowledgments

The authors are indebted to the teachers and administrative staff of Discovery Preschool, Peoria, Illinois; West Liberty Dual Language Prekindergarten Program, West Liberty, Iowa; Rockford Early Childhood Program, Rockford, Illinois; and Rock Island Head Start Program, Rock Island, Illinois, for their support during the writing of the initial book, *Teaching Your Child to Love Learning*. The authors also wish to thank the Rock Island Regional Office of Education, Partnering with Parents/Early Learning Quad Cities, and Family and Classroom Educational Support Program, Edwardsville Public Schools for field testing the manual and providing the additional projects for the CD.

PART I

Introduction to Family Projects and the Tool Kit

The Project Approach for Parents

The Project Approach for Parents?

We came together to write *Teaching Your Child to Love Learning: A Guide to Doing Projects at Home* because we recognized a need for parents to know more about how to support their children's learning within the home environment. While teaching and directing programs for young children, we found the project approach to be a meaningful and effective way to organize teaching experiences. When a project was going on in a classroom, we found the level of involvement of children, teachers, and parents increased.

During project work we were able to realize our ideal image of learning experiences as intellectually stimulating adventures and our ideal image of schools and centers as communities of learners. We found in our own parenting that in our richest vacations, family experiences, and family projects we were utilizing methods and techniques from the project approach. Shaping experiences into projects became a way to organize materials, motivate us as parents to support our children's learning, create lasting memories with our children, and build strong relationships.

About 10 years ago, a workshop series for parents on the project approach was developed for an urban preschool program for children at risk of academic failure. The project approach provided a structure—a way for parents to learn techniques to support their children's learning. That series was well received by the parents. As we moved onto other jobs with other programs, we continued our project work in the classroom and in our own homes, but not with parents. Our interest in parents and project work emerged again when we had an opportunity to open a Reggio-inspired, faith-based preschool program. Although these parents were well-educated, we saw that sup-porting their children's interest and connecting with children in meaningful, developmental ways was a challenge for these parents also.

For all parents, regardless of location, income, education, culture, or ethnic background, connecting with children in ways that enable them to become enthusiastic learners is a challenge. We found that parents want their children to excel, but have many questions about how to do that. Should they buy videotapes of alphabet songs, sign them up for every class they can get them into, buy educational toys, or provide a computer? We also found that parents have concerns about what are appropriate activities for each age level. They are also confused about the best way to support their child's learning, either feeling like they have to become school teachers or hesitant to teach their child anything. They are confused about their role and how to coach their child. We also found that many parents are concerned about making and maintaining emotional connections with their children. They want to find a meaningful way in their busy lives to relate to their children, but aren't exactly sure how to do that.

What Are the Benefits to Children from Doing Projects?

- Children have a reason to learn and practice academic skills.
- Children develop positive dispositions toward learning.
- Children develop self-esteem because they build competence.
- Children learn democratic values as they learn to appreciate what work people do.
- Children strengthen their capacity to wonder.

What Are the Benefits to Parents of Doing Projects with Their Children?

- Because the project has a timeline and immediacy, parents make time for their child.
- Parents become partners in their child's learning, not only by providing a role model of a learner but also by learning and expanding their own knowledge.
- Parents learn the strengths, talents, approaches to learning, sense of humor, and depth of knowledge and skills of their children.
- Parents strengthen their relationship with other family members.

How Do Parents Learn How to Use the Project Approach at Home?

The book *Teaching Your Child to Love Learning: A Guide to Doing Projects at Home* provides a guide for parents who are frequent readers. There are, however, many other parents who would benefit from learning this technique. This *Tool Kit* was created to help the staff of schools, early childhood programs, home visitor programs, community services, and family literacy organizations bring these ideas to the parents in their programs. There are also organizations who provide training to home child-care providers or to home schoolers who could use the ideas we present.

Parents can learn to do projects through

- **Independent reading** of *Teaching Your Child to Love Learning* and completion of the Family Project Planning Journal
- **Book study groups** on *Teaching Your Child to Love Learning* at libraries, churches, schools, child-care centers, or community agencies.
- **Workshop series** in which parents complete a project at home using the book as a text and share their progress with the group
- **Home-visitor programs** in which the home-visitor shares techniques and methods from the *Tool Kit* and *Teaching Your Child to Love Learning*
- **Focused meetings** during a school year as part of a parent education component of an early childhood program for children at risk

- **Family-literacy component** where learning to coach project work can be part of Parent and Child Together (PACT) experiences
- **Home schooling support groups** where home schooling parents can use project work as a way to integrate learning experiences for their children.

This Tool Kit Provides the Following Resources:

- Syllabi and agendas for parent workshops
- Talks: Outlines and handouts for informal talks
- Activities for parent workshops
- Photocopy masters for the Family Project Planning Journal in English and Spanish
- A CD with PowerPoint® talks on key phases of project work, PowerPoint® presentations on projects featured in *Teaching Your Child to Love Learning*, and PowerPoint® presentations of additional projects collected from diverse family groups using the workshop materials

Using the Tool Kit

The *Tool Kit* is organized around four units of study:

1. Getting Ready for Project Work
2. Selecting a Topic and Beginning Investigation
3. Investigation and Representation
4. Sharing and Celebrating Projects

Facilitators are encouraged to use these tools flexibly to match the needs of the parents. Suggested agendas are provided for a workshop series along with variations for making the experience positive for different groups. PowerPoint® presentations may be shared using a computer and LCD projector, printed on a color printer as color transparencies, or printed on a color printer as individual slides and assembled to make Project History Books to share with parents.

The Family Project Planning Journal from *Teaching Your Child to Love Learning* is included in large format at the end of the *Tool Kit*. It can be photocopied and given to parents in a binder.

A Spanish version of the Family Project Planning Journal is also provided in large format for Spanish-speaking parents, along with translations of handouts for activities.

Using the Units of Study

There are four units of study with *Talks, Activities,* and *PowerPoint® Presentations* for each unit. Facilitators are encouraged to arrange the study of these units according to the needs of the adults within the group. We provide sample agendas and syllabi for four sessions over a 6- or 7-week workshop series. Facilitators may instead plan on spending one, two, or more sessions on each unit. The units may be subdivided for extended programs or programs that meet over the school year. Here are some variations.

Library Adult–Child Class

Teaching Your Child to Love Learning: A Guide to Doing Projects at Home can be used for adult–child classes or summer programs at libraries. Parents, grandparents, or even babysitters could participate with a child. The emphasis on research, literacy, and the use of books makes it a good introduction for children of preschool and early elementary school age to the benefits of libraries. The four units can be the focus of a 4 or 6-week meeting period with each family choosing a topic and doing the investigation and representation. A closing event could be a display of documentation at the library. It takes approximately 6 weeks to do a project with in-depth investigation, so we recommend having the class meet over this time period. We recommend a 1½-hour meeting time with children occupied part of the time in a story session or, depending on the age group, looking at books related to their project topic so that adults can meet together and discuss *Teaching Your Child to Love Learning* and project issues.

Family Literacy Programs

Projects are an excellent option for parent-and-child-together activities in family literacy programs. The nature of project work requires the use of books, writing, and communicating. Children and adults learn new vocabulary. Activities teach parents how to observe children's development, provide appropriate feedback, and coach children in academic skills. The Family Project Planning Journal can be used by parents to keep track of projects and also as a journal. Adaptations of activities for family literacy programs are included in project descriptions, and a simplified flowchart is provided. The making of project history books is an effective way to document project work and involve children and adults in writing and creating books together. The activities in the four units can be spaced throughout several months; then additional planning journals can be copied for subsequent projects.

Families with Limited Income

Family projects can be an addition to programs for families with limited incomes. The provision of project kits to families as part of class work brings writing and art materials into the home and provides a place to keep things together. Doing projects with children emphasizes the strengths of both parents and children. Because projects are focused on what interests children in their everyday lives, they are usually culturally relevant to the child. Selecting topics with which parents have familiarity means that they can support their children's learning. In the process of doing projects, parents will learn how to support their child's research efforts and where resources can be found at little cost within the community. Helping a child successfully complete a project builds confidence in all family members. Specific ideas for involving families with limited income are included on the next pages.

Second Language Learners

Project work can be an effective addition to programs for second language learners. Because topics focus on children's lives and familiar places, it provides an opportunity for all family members to interact with the community. Project work builds vocabulary as children learn the names of parts of things, processes, and locations. Reading and writing can be done in both the home language and the second language. Project history books are an excellent way to stimulate the use of a second language. Materials for Spanish speakers are provided in this *Tool Kit*. They consist of the Family Project Planning Journal that can be copied and put in notebooks for parents and handouts required for the activities.

Parent Workshop Organization

We have found that a class of four 2-hour sessions spread over 6–8 weeks enables parents to complete a project and share it with other participants. Parents appear to be willing to commit to four sessions for a voluntary workshop. We have divided the training activities into four units. When used in conjunction with a family literacy program or home-visiting program, activities for each unit can be spread over a longer period of time. Facilitators should feel free to divide units to meet the needs of their parents.

It is not always easy to get parents to commit to workshops or activities with their children. We have found these ideas helpful:

1. Send home a brochure with pictures of children doing fun projects.
2. Repeat distribution of the brochure for several weeks if the initial response is lower than expected.
3. Feature food and fun activities.
4. If materials and supplies will be provided, tell what the parents will receive.
5. Pass out brochures and put up posters at other group gatherings (e.g., open houses, parent-teacher conferences, fundraisers).
6. Be willing to run the first class with low enrollment to develop a reputation.
7. Consider what would be an appropriate time of the year for the class. Stay away from busy holiday times.
8. Don't offer the class until families have a chance to settle in to school routines.
9. Look for non-busy times (summer may work well, or January through March)
10. Consider the best time of day and day of the week to offer classes. This information could be collected through a class survey, at school registration, parent-teacher conferences, or through informal conversations with parents. (Some families may find early evening with informal supper most convenient; on the other hand, in some families the dinner hour is always spent at home. In some communities certain nights are reserved for religious activities.)
11. Open the class to parents from other groups. Join with another teacher, grade level, or center.
12. Individually invite parents—face to face or by phone—and tell them the names of other parents who have already signed up.
13. Feature the class in classroom newsletters, school news in the local paper, and district newsletters.
14. Make posters about the class. Feature children's projects in the posters. (This is especially helpful if you are currently doing project work in your school or center or if you have project documentation from previous family project classes. If not, pictures can be printed from the presentations on the CD.)
15. Tell children about the class, and ask them to talk to their parents.
16. Provide free child care during the class time. This can often be done with high school students participating as a service project. PTA association or parent board members may also volunteer to support the project class by providing child care. Child care by support staff may be an allowable expense in parent education grants.

GETTING STARTED

Establishing a Rapport and Setting an Informal Atmosphere at the Very First Meeting

Send reminders home before the first class so no one misses the first meeting

- Remind parents orally if you see them at the center or school.
- Call to remind parents.
- Be friendly and relaxed with your group.
- Use first names including your own, if culturally appropriate. Have nametags prepared.
- Give a background of yourself and your own experiences as a child or doing projects with children.
- Provide food or snacks if the class occurs in early evening. In some classes this may be done on a rotating basis.
- Provide notebooks for keeping notes, agendas, and handouts for the group, and include a pen.
- Provide labeling cards for their supplies at home.
- Provide a break during the sessions so that the group can get snacks and mingle.

Using Teaching Technology That Is Comfortable for Your Families

Think of the comfort level of your families with schooling and school traditions. As you decide how to use the presentations and choose activities, consider your audience's comfort and confidence with technology.

Some parents will enjoy seeing you use an LCD projector and show the PowerPoint® presentations. Others might feel that this is too intimidating, too school-like. You might want to use an overhead projector or just write notes on a flip chart. Activities coordinate with assigned readings in *Teaching Your Child to Love Learning*; however, you may find it more practical for you to read the book and share the contents with your group. Be careful when talking about using the internet at home—never assume that there is a computer or access to the internet within every home unless you know your parents.

Variations for Family Literacy Programs

1. Reading activities. Observe the groups when you give a reading task, and be sure to allow enough time to read and discuss (for example, reading the project summaries). You may want to have more confident readers read to the group during some activities.

Feel free to rewrite directions or to alter activity worksheets to match the vocabulary or cultural background of your group.

2. Writing activities. Consider the comfort level of participants in spelling or writing in front of a group. For some group activities, the leader might volunteer to write what the participants say.

When using the Family Project Planning Journal, we have found it helpful to emphasize that the journaling is private—it doesn't matter if spelling is correct. State that there is no grade given for the class.

3. Speaking before a group. If participants are not comfortable sharing with the whole group, divide them into smaller groups to share, or into pairs.

IDEAS FOR INVOLVING FAMILIES WITH LIMITED INCOME

Most projects do not require a lot of money. Activities such as inspecting the inside of a truck, visiting the store rooms of a grocery store, or going to the library to look for books about butterflies cost nothing. When parents do projects, they discover that there are many fun things they can do with their child that do not cost money. They are also learning how to support their children's educational development. If art and writing materials such as paper, pencils, paint, and poster board are in the home, parents can encourage children to represent their learning and practice literacy and other school skills.

When introducing projects to families with limited income, providing access to materials for project work will not only encourage project work but will also enrich the educational environment for the children in the home. Having these materials increases the likelihood that parents will bring more school-related skills into project work, and encourages continuation of activities after the project class is completed. We have found that assembling materials into a kit for each family encourages attendance and parent and child involvement in the project.

We have also found it helpful to provide free child care for evening or after-school workshops. Child care during parent workshops can be a problem for parents with limited income. The workshop may be organized so that children join parents for part of the session, especially the last session when projects are shared. For some programs, daytime classes while children are in classrooms can be provided by librarians or other support staff.

With a little bit of planning, parent workshops can be used to introduce families to free public resources in their community. As families begin to investigate and identify questions, they will be motivated to find answers to these questions. It is helpful to have a workshop session at the library or to go to the library as a field-trip for the project class. In addition to children's books on the topic, the library will also have adult books with photos and diagrams, and periodicals that might be helpful. If families do not have internet access in the home, they can learn how to access the internet through their public library. If you call in advance, a librarian will be happy to set up an orientation to their services, including the internet, and also get them signed up for library cards if they don't have them.

If time permits and the ages of the children are similar, another meeting with the children can be scheduled at the library, with all participants doing research on their topic at the same time. Talking in advance to the librarian about the topics the chil-

dren are researching and some of their questions will maximize the effectiveness of the time at the library and insure that the library experience is successful.

Suggested Family Project Kit

Plastic storage tub (approximately 5 U.S. gallons)
Paper (construction, tablets, colored paper, blank white paper)
Blank file cards for making word cards
Glue
Watercolor paints
Small set of tempera paints
Modeling clay
Child-size scissors
Crayons
Disposable camera (Collect and develop the photos or make arrangements for a store to develop them and bill you directly.)
Poster Board—for last session displays

In addition to the project kit, provide copies of the Family Project Planning Journal in a three-ring binder and materials for the parents to use in workshops. If your families are readers, it is helpful to also provide individual copies of *Teaching Your Child to Love Learning*.

Sample Workshop Agendas

UNIT 1
Getting Ready for Project Work

This is a sample agenda for a 2-hour basic workshop session.

Goals

- To share the benefit of project work with parents
- To introduce the concept of projects and the phases to parents
- To show how parents can organize their homes to maximize learning experiences

Outline

Facilitators should feel free to reorganize this outline or choose what they wish to use. There is no break, but during a small group activity parents can move about and pick up a snack.

0:00–0:15	Welcome (see expanded guidelines on next page).
0:15–0:45	*Talk:* Why Do Projects with Your Children? *PowerPoint® Presentation:* Maude the Dog (Optional PowerPoint® Presentation: Flow Chart of Family Projects)
0:45–1:00	*Group Activity*: read a project summary *There are several summaries available, you may select by age level or by topic.*
1:00–1:20	Introduction to Project Journal *Pass out journals and walk through journal pointing out features and phases.*
1:20–1:50	*PowerPoint® Presentation:* Setting the Stage for Learning *The facilitator may just talk through this information, which is in Chapter 2.*
1:50–2:00	Assignment for next time: *Teaching Your Child to Love Learning:* Read Chapters 1, 2, & 3. Family Project Planning Journal: Complete pages 2, 3, 4, 5, 6, 10, & 11. Observe their children and make a list of what things interest them.

Introduction to the Group

Goal

- To introduce facilitators to the group and participants to each other.
- To set the stage for sharing project experiences with each other.

Time Frame

This activity should take no more than 15 minutes of the 2-hour time period.

Materials

Nametags for each participant. If these are adhesive name tags that are not reusable these should be available also for the second session or until the facilitator thinks everyone knows everyone else. If there is a large group the facilitator may want to consider reusable nametags (pin-on or hanging) that can be collected at the end of the session and redistributed each time.

Large chart paper tacked on board and marker for facilitator to record name of parent with the name and ages of their children for everyone to see. This can be copied onto a handout to be given to parents for the next session.

Activity

Introduce yourself as facilitator and any other helpers who will be in the class. Then ask the parents to introduce themselves to the group. To get the class moving quickly, encourage parents to be brief. You can specify what they are to say by giving them three points to remember:

1. Name—if it is a couple, one person can introduce the couple
2. Names of their children and ages
3. Why they want to take the class

As the parents introduce themselves, write the names of each parent and each child and age level of each child on the chart paper in some organized fashion. Be sure to have looked at a class list first so that you will know how to spell the parent's (or grandparent's) names correctly. If you have access in advance to the names of the children, look at these also.

Tell the group you will give them a copy of this list next time so that they can all get to know each other.

Optional: Make this list have four columns: Adult's name, Children's names, Children's interests, and Projects. Fill in only the first two columns at this session. At Session 2, fill in column three, and at Session 3, fill in column 4.

UNIT 2
Selecting a Topic and Beginning to Investigate

This is a sample agenda for a two hour basic workshop session.

Goals

- To provide criteria for selecting topics
- To discuss children's interests and possible project topics from those interests
- To introduce parents to investigation activities

Outline

Facilitators should feel free to reorganize this outline or choose what they wish to use. There is no break, but during a small group activity parents can move about and pick up a snack.

0:00–0:05	Welcome back, introduce any participants who missed the first session.
0:05–0:55	*Talk:* What Makes a Good Project Topic?
	Activity: Choosing the Best Topic
0:15–0:45	Discussion of observations of children's interests and possible topics
0:45–1:00	*PowerPoint® Presentation:* The Race Car Project
1:00–1:35	*PowerPoint® Presentation:* Introduction to Investigation and Representation
1:35–1:55	Review of Project Journal and Talk about Messing Around with Topic
1:55–2:00	Assignment for next time:
	Teaching Your Child to Love Learning: Read Chapters 4, 5, & 7
	Family Project Planning Journal: Complete pages 7, 8, & 9
	Mess around with a topic with their children and consider how they might investigate it.

UNIT 3
Investigation and Representation

This is a sample agenda for a 2-hour basic workshop session.

Goals

- To enable parents to share where they are in the project process
- To discuss children's responses
- To introduce parents to investigation activities

Outline

Facilitators should feel free to reorganize this outline or choose what they wish to use. There is no break, but during a small group activity parents can move about and pick up a snack.

Time	Activity
0:00—0:10	*Activity:* What Phase Are You In? *Parents put sticker on the flowchart to indicate where they are on the progress of their project.*
0:10–0:40	*Activity:* Ask each family to share progress
0:40–0:55	***PowerPoint® Presentation:*** Mexican Bakery Project or The Bus Project
0:55–1:10	*Activity:* Sketching Keys or Representation Experience for Parents
1:10–1:40	*Talk:* Stages of Representation / *Talk:* Principles of Coaching
1:40–1:55	If this is the next to last session—***PowerPoint® Presentation:*** Celebrating the Learning *Provide instructions on display and sharing of projects for last session.* If not the next to last session—*Activity:* Effective Coaching During Project Work
1:55–2:00	Assignment for next time: *Teaching Your Child to Love Learning:* Read Chapters 6 & 8 Family Project Planning Journal: Complete pages 12–18 Request that parents share where they are on their project during the final meeting time. Be sure to let parents know that projects don't have to be done at that time.

UNIT 4
Sharing and Celebrating Projects

This is a sample agenda for a 2-hour basic workshop session.

Goals

- To enable parents to share the projects
- To discuss children's responses to project work
- To introduce parents to ways of documenting and sharing

This may be the last session. Children may be included for part of the session. One way to do this would be to have child care for the first hour of the session and then have children join the class when the projects are shared

Outline

Facilitators should feel free to reorganize this outline or choose what they wish to use. There is no break but during a small group activity parents can move about and pick up a snack.

0:00–0:10   If this is the last session—***Activity:*** Set Up Project Documentation
As parents enter, have a location for them to place their projects. Have poster board available if parents have things they would like to stick up. Using double stick tape will make this process go quickly.
If this is not the last session—***PowerPoint® Presentation:*** Celebrating the Learning

0:10–0:20   ***Group Activity:*** Reflecting on Project Work Using the Question List
Use the list of questions for discussion. Facilitators may pass them out, put them on an overhead, or copy them onto chart paper. Be sure to encourage all participants to share their thoughts on at least some of the questions.
Pass out the List of Questions for Discussion
If this is not the last session—***Activity:*** Documenting Children's Learning

0:20–1:55   ***Group Activity:*** Sharing projects
Take turns having each parent share their projects. Divide the time available for sharing by the number of projects to be shared. Set a time limit and appoint a time keeper. Provide the handout for sharing so that parents can organize their thoughts
If this is not the last session—***PowerPoint® Presentation:*** The Horse Project and one other project of choice

1:55–2:00   Closing
Pass out evaluations and ask for feedback
Thank everyone for attending

Flyer for workshop series:

1. Cover these instructions.
2. Make a double-sided copy of this page and the following page.
3. Add in information regarding class dates, times, and how to register.
4. Fold in thirds.
5. Distribute to parents.

A GUIDE TO DOING PROJECTS AT HOME

Teaching Your Child to Love Learning

Judy Harris Helm
Stacy Berg
Pam Scranton

Teaching Your Child To Love Learning

A Guide to Doing Projects at Home

A class for parents, grandparents, and caregivers

For questions, contact

About
TEACHING YOUR CHILD
TO LOVE LEARNING

Doing projects with your children at home is a way for parents, grandparents, or caregivers to support their children's growth and development in fun ways. When children do a project about a topic of interest, they

- Have a reason to practice academic skills like reading, writing, and doing numbers
- Develop dispositions to want to learn, to be curious, and to solve problems
- Develop self-esteem by reaching their own goals
- Develop an appreciation for others, the work they do, and how everyone contributes to society
- Experience awe and wonder as they learn about the natural world
- As a helper in your child's project work you will
  —Make quality time for your child
  —Become a partner in your child's learning
  —Strengthen family relationships
  —Learn coaching skills that will enable you to help your child throughout school

When children know you care about their learning, they are more likely to become eager learners. Together you can share something special.

Class Dates
and Times

Session dates:

These classes will introduce families to project work in the home using *Teaching Your Child to Love Learning*. Participants will discover the joys of creating an environment for meaningful learning, encouraging children's representations, incorporating academic skills within the investigations, and planning a celebration at the end of the project.

For questions, contact:

Registration

Submit registration form to:

Name:		
Address:		
City:	State:	Zip:
Phone:		
Email address:		

Moving On Down the Road

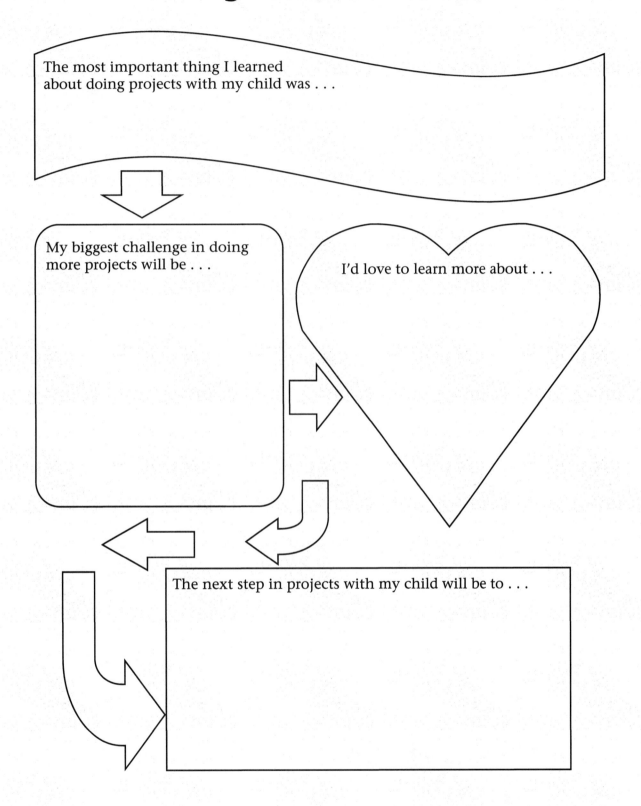

The most important thing I learned about doing projects with my child was . . .

My biggest challenge in doing more projects will be . . .

I'd love to learn more about . . .

The next step in projects with my child will be to . . .

PART II

Units of Study:
Talks, Activities, and
PowerPoint® Presentations

Overview of Units

Unit	Book Background (*Teaching Your Child to Love Learning*)	Talks	PowerPoint® Presentations	Activities	Assignments
1. Getting Ready for Work	Chapters 1, 2, & 3	Why Do Projects with Your Children?	Flowchart of Family Projects Setting the Stage Maude the Dog	Reading Project Summaries	Chapters 1, 2, & 3 Journal pages 2–6, 10, & 11
2. Selecting a Topic and Beginning Investigation	Chapters 4 & 5 Chapter 7 on Child's Development may also be read during this time	What Makes a Good Project Topic?	Race Care Project Introduction to Investigation and Representation	Choosing the Best Topic Reporting on Children's Interests Using a Web to Find Out What Children Know	Chapters 4, 5, & 7 (7 optional) Journal pages 7–9
3. Investigation and Representation	Chapters 7, 8, & 9	Stages of Representation Principles of Coaching	Mexican Bakery Project The Bus Project Celebrating the Learning (if next session is last session)	What Phase Are You In? Sketching Keys Representation Experience for Parents Effective Coaching During Project Work	Chapters 6 & 8 Journal pages 12–17 as needed (Assign page 18 if next session is last session)
4. Celebrating Project Work	Chapter 6		Celebrating the Learning The Horse Project	Documenting Children's Learning During Project Work Reflecting on Project Work Sharing of Project Documentation	Complete Journal pages 19 & 20

UNIT 1

Getting Ready for Project Work

TALK
Why Do Projects with Your Children?

Directions for Facilitators

This talk should be done informally by the facilitator. The main point you want to make is that project work will benefit their children and that they as parents (or grandparents or caregivers) will find that project work benefits them also. This talk should be given before *Teaching Your Child to Love Learning* is distributed. Share your own experiences doing project work or project-like activities with children. Encourage parents to talk about project-like experiences they had as children such as building a tree house, putting on a circus show, or creating their own club. If appropriate, talk about how children are often not able to have these experiences because of safety in the neighborhood, spending time in group care, or lack of playmates.

Prepare for this talk by reading Chapter 1 in *Teaching Your Child to Love Learning*

Main Points for Talk

Doing projects with children at home is a way for parents, grandparents, or caregivers to support their children's growth and development in fun ways.

When children do a project about a topic of interest, they:

- Have a reason to practice academic skills like reading, writing, and doing numbers
- Develop dispositions to want to learn, to be curious, and to solve problems
- Develop self-esteem by reaching their own goals
- Develop an appreciation for others, the work they do, and how everyone contributes to society
- Experience awe and wonder as they learn about the natural world

As a helper in your child's project work, you will:

- Make quality time for your child
- Become a partner in your child's learning
- Strengthen family relationships
- Learn coaching skills that will enable you to help your child throughout school

Stress that when children know that parents care about their learning, they are more likely to become eager learners. Together they can share special time and build memories with their children, and also increase their parenting skills.

POWERPOINT® PRESENTATION
FLOWCHART OF FAMILY PROJECTS

Directions for Facilitators

This information can be shared informally using the flowchart diagram instead of the PowerPoint® presentation if desired.

Pass out copies of the flowchart or turn to page 40 of *Teaching Your Child to Love Learning*, or the first page of the Family Project Planning Journal.

By talking through this flowchart you will be introducing parents to the following:

- There is a flow or structure to project work—this not only guides you but also motivates you to keep moving on your project.
- Family projects, like projects in classrooms, have three parts called phases.
- The three phases of family projects are:
  - Beginning the project
  - Investigating
  - Celebrating
- Some projects last a long time (months), and some only for a few weeks.

Variation for Family Literacy Programs

Use the Flowchart for Family Literacy, which requires a lower reading level.

Variation for Spanish Speakers

Use the Flowchart on page 3 in the Spanish Family Project Planning Journal at the back of this tool kit.

POWERPOINT® PRESENTATION
FLOWCHART OF FAMILY PROJECTS

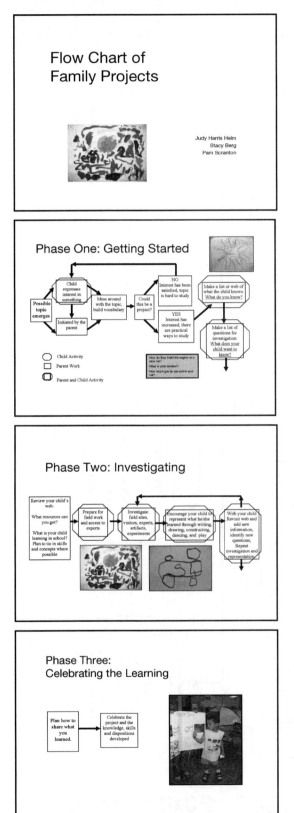

This PowerPoint® presentation
* Illustrates progression of phases of a project
* Uses the Race Car Project as an illustration

This PowerPoint® presentation is animated. Each click will advance to the next step in the flowchart. The flowchart is reproduced at the beginning of the Family Project Planning Journal and may be copied for a handout.

This PowerPoint® presentation can also be printed on a color printer to make transparencies.

Phase One is the beginning of a project. Point out the legend. Octagon shapes are child activities and rectangles are parent activities. When these shapes are combined, they indicate shared activities. As you discuss this flowchart, talk about how topics can emerge from a child's interest or can be initiated by the parent. Stress the importance of messing around with the topic. Note that there may be a number of possible topics before one emerges that sustains interest.

Phase Two: Investigating. Talk about how children learn through investigation, then represent what they learned, then develop more questions, followed by more representation, etc. This phase ends when children begin to lose interest or resources are exhausted.

Phase Three: Celebrating the Learning. Emphasize the importance of celebrating with your child. Remind parents that the goals of developing positive dispositions for learning and building self-confidence are enhanced when they take time to celebrate with the child. (These goals are discussed on pages 12 and 13 of *Teaching Your Child to Love Learning*.)

Flowchart of Family Projects

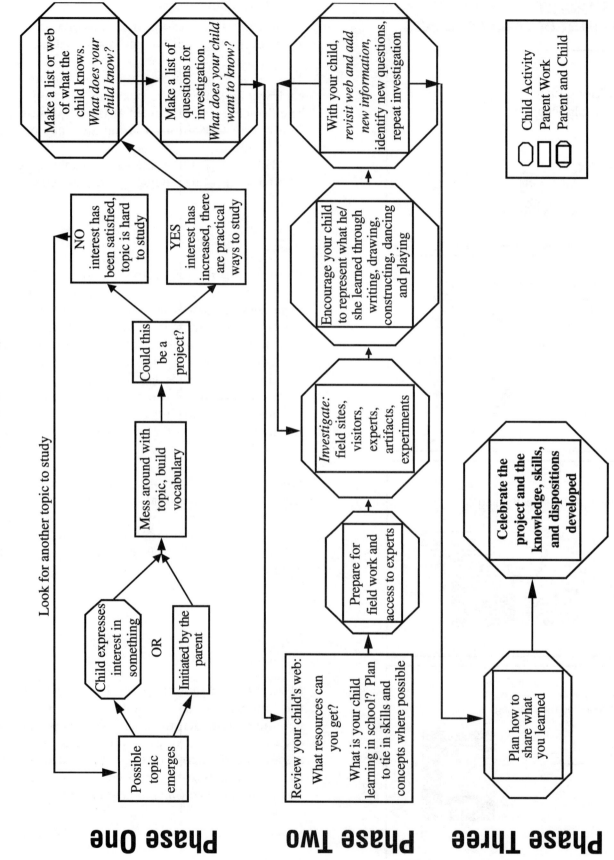

Phase One

Look for another topic to study

- Make a list or web of what the child knows. *What does your child know?*
- Make a list of questions for investigation. *What does your child want to know?*

- NO interest has been satisfied, topic is hard to study
- YES interest has increased, there are practical ways to study

- Could this be a project?
- Mess around with topic, build vocabulary
- Child expresses interest in something OR Initiated by the parent
- Possible topic emerges

Phase Two

- With your child, *revisit web and add new information*, identify new questions, repeat investigation
- Encourage your child to represent what he/she learned through writing, drawing, constructing, dancing and playing
- *Investigate:* field sites, visitors, experts, artifacts, experiments
- Prepare for field work and access to experts
- Review your child's web: What resources can you get? What is your child learning in school? Plan to tie in skills and concepts where possible

Phase Three

- Celebrate the project and the knowledge, skills, and dispositions developed
- Plan how to share what you learned

Child Activity
Parent Work
Parent and Child

Flowchart of Family Projects

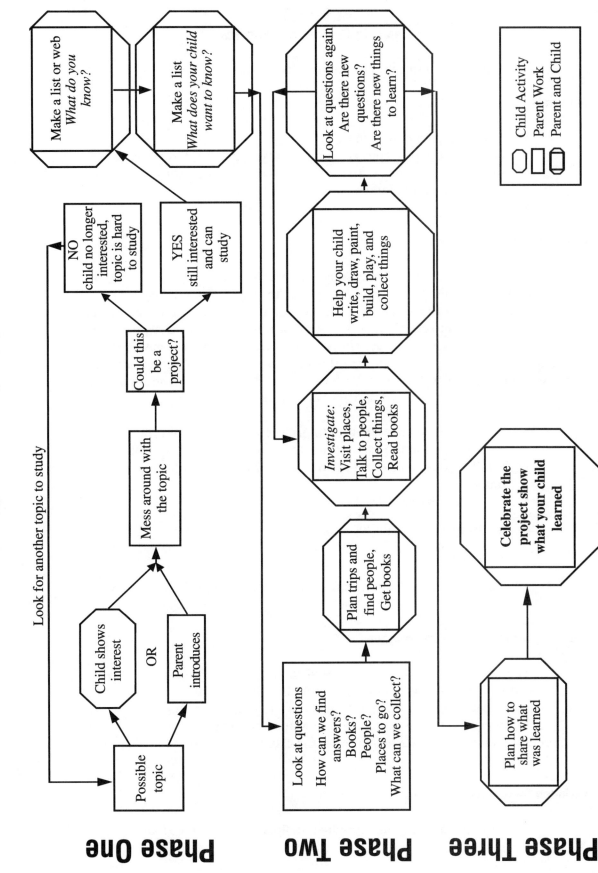

Phase One

Possible topic

Child shows interest OR Parent introduces

Mess around with the topic

Could this be a project?

NO child no longer interested, topic is hard to study

YES still interested and can study

Make a list or web *What do you know?*

Make a list *What does your child want to know?*

Look for another topic to study

Phase Two

Look at questions How can we find answers? Books? People? Places to go? What can we collect?

Plan trips and find people, Get books

Investigate: Visit places, Talk to people, Collect things, Read books

Help your child write, draw, paint, build, play, and collect things

Look at questions again Are there new questions? Are there new things to learn?

Phase Three

Plan how to share what was learned

Celebrate the project show what your child learned

Child Activity
Parent Work
Parent and Child

ACTIVITY
Reading Project Summaries

Three project summaries are provided for your use

Materials

- Copies of project flowchart
- Copies of the three project summaries on the next few pages (These may be color-coded, collected, and used again for another group)
- Chart paper and markers
- Tape to post chart paper at close of activity

Directions for Facilitators

Divide the group into small groups of two, three, or four participants. Pass out copies of the flowchart handout or refer to page 40 of *Teaching Your Child to Love Learning* or to the copy on page 3 of Family Project Planning Journal.

Each group is to choose a project summary, get a piece of chart paper, and divide it into three parts. They will label the parts Phase One, Phase Two, and Phase Three. Each group will read the summary they have chosen and then list the main events during each phase on the chart. While reading and discussing the project summaries, parents will learn the following:

- There is a flow or a structure to project work—this not only guides parents but also motivates them to keep moving on the project.
- Family projects, like projects in classrooms, have three parts called phases.
- The three phases of family projects are:
  — Beginning the project
  — Investigating
  — Celebrating
- Some projects last a long time (months) and some only for a few weeks.

Variation for Family Literacy Programs

The facilitator may read the titles of the projects to the class, and let the class choose which description they would like the facilitator to read to them. The participants can tell the main events in the project by phases.

Another variation is to review the Maude the Dog Project PowerPoint® presentation and have participants list the events that occurred in each phase of this project.

Variation for Spanish Speakers

The project summaries are provided in Spanish on pages 31–34.

The Shoe Project
2-Year-Old Girl and Her Single Mom

Phase One: Getting Started

A 2-year-old girl was playing in her mommy's closet and putting on all of her shoes. The mom noticed she was interested in shoes, and she started pointing out other people's shoes when they shopped at the grocery store. On a Saturday, the mom and child went to the library and checked out a book about shoes. The pair read the book over and over, and the child began to repeat words like *boots*, *slippers*, and *light-up shoes*. Up in the bedroom, the mom pulled out 10 shoes, and they played a matching game with the pairs. Next they put mom's shoes and the toddler's shoes together and sorted them into a pile of little shoes and a pile of big shoes.

Phase Two: Investigating

The mom noticed that the toddler has outgrown her current tennis shoes and planned a trip to Payless. At the store, the mom began measuring the toddler's foot with the metal foot measurer. The mom showed the toddler her choices of tennis shoes in her size. After the toddler selected the princess tennis shoes, the mom played a few learning games with the toddler. They found boots, dress-up shoes, tennis shoes, slippers, and light-up shoes. They hunted for the toddler's favorite characters on shoes, including Elmo and Teletubbies. As they checked out, the mom allowed the toddler to give the cashier the money. After they returned home, the mom took ads from the Sunday paper and helped the toddler point to pictures of different shoes. Then she cut out the shoe pictures and made a book for her daughter. The mom also collected a variety of shoes in a crate for her daughter to play with independently.

Phase Three: Celebrating

To share the project, the mom took the toddler to Grandma's house to show her the new shoes and the shoe book. Grandma and the toddler looked at the book a number of times together. The toddler remembered many of the words from the book. After reading the book, Grandma showed the toddler the shoes in her closet.

27

The Garage Project
4-Year-Old Boy and His Father

Phase One: Getting Started

A four-year-old boy watched as his father checked the brake lights and the air in the tires. He asked his daddy what he was doing. The father showed him how the air came out of the tire by guiding his son's hand near the stem. The father showed the son how the air made a measurement on the tire gauge. The father then checked the brake lights and turn signals. The father let his son press the brake pedal and turn on the signal lights. Sensing an interest from all of his son's questions, the father opened the hood of the car and let his son ask additional questions. The son wanted to know "What's this?" and "What's that?," pointing to each item. The father pulled out the dipstick and showed his son how he knew the car needed more oil. As they went into the house, the little boy ran to his mother to tell her all about what he had seen. The mother picked up a pen and paper and told her son she wanted to write down some of the things he had learned. As the mother wrote down her son's thoughts, the father went back out to the car to get the car's manual. Together the father and son looked at the pictures in the owner's manual. At dinner, the father suggested that it was time to get the oil changed and that maybe the son could go with him. After dinner, father and son made a list of three questions they could ask the mechanic.

Phase Two: Investigating

A couple of days later, the father called The Grease Spot to see if he and his son could watch as the oil was being changed. The father also shared his son's questions with the mechanic and the mechanic agreed to have someone answer the child's questions. The following Saturday, father and son visited The Grease Spot. The mechanic answered the questions, "Where does the old oil go?" and "What do the numbers mean?" (on the side of the oil can). The mechanic also showed the boy an old air filter. As he was paying, the father picked up several brochures which included a picture of the building and men working on cars. After returning home, the little boy ran to get his hot wheels and used blocks to build ramps. The boy drew a picture of the garage and the cars over the wells. The father noticed the boy representing what he had learned, and he suggested to the boy that they might build a garage using a cardboard box. The father asked his son what he would like to include in the garage and made a list of what he said. He then asked his son how he would create the items on the list for the garage. "What will you need to do that?" asked the father. The father and son worked on the project off-and-on for a week, collecting a variety of items for the garage. Blocks were used to make ramps for the cars and the father cut the doors where the boy suggested. The boy made a sign out of an old envelope and some windows for the building out of Saran wrap. Each time the son finished one part, the father referred to the list and asked the child how he was going to add the next part. As the building developed, the son continued to play with his cars in the garage.

Phase Three: Celebrating

As the garage was completed, the father asked his son whom he would like to share this with. The son decided to invite cousin Joey and Uncle Earl over to the house to see the completed project so he could tell them all about what he had learned. The boys played a long time with the cars and the garage. The father listened to their conversation and heard his son use many words he had learned during the project. Before the guests left, Joey said, "Hey, where you are going to wash these cars?" The little boy looked at his father and said, "Let's go to the car wash!"

The Big Machine Project
4- and 6-Year-Old Boys and Their Mom

Phase One: Getting Started

After moving into a new housing development, two brothers were very interested in all of the big machines they saw working around them. Each day they would watch the machines at work and try to name them and talked about what they did. At times the brothers disagreed, and discussions became heated. To turn their interest in a positive direction, the mother suggested that each boy choose a particular machine about which to become an expert. To help the children make an educated choice, she gathered any books from their bedroom about big machines, and they read one book per night, discussing the choices. On Friday the older son chose the bulldozer and the younger son chose the cement mixer to study. On Saturday morning, the mother took her sons to the library to find resources about their specific machines.

Phase Two: Investigating

To begin the investigation, the mom asked the boys to make a list of three things they knew about their machine and three things they wanted to know about their machine. Later in the week the mother and sons took a walk and watched the machines at work. The children each took pictures of their machine. When a worker was available, she asked if the boys could come and ask their questions the next day. After the film was developed, with the mother's help, each boy made a simple book using his pictures. Some pictures went with the things the boys knew, and some were used for the new things they had learned. The mom also incorporated the machines into other activities. For an art project, the mom provided the boys with mud like they had seen the bulldozer push to paint pictures. She also helped them make plaster of Paris (similar to the concrete the mixer had poured) to make prints of their hands in plastic containers. She gathered their toy tractors and added them to their sandbox.

Phase Three: Celebrating

To share the project, the boys invited a few friends over for a big machine party. The books they made were shared, as well as the ones they had collected from their room and from the library. The children played out in the sandbox with the tractors and made pictures using wheel tracks of machines and other tractors. The children finished the party with a cake decorated with help from the boys featuring each of their machines.

El proyecto de los zapatos
Una niña de 2 años y su mamá

Primera fase: Comenzar

Una niña de 2 años estaba jugando en el armario de su mamá, poniéndose todos los zapatos de su mamá. La mamá se dio cuenta que la niña tenía interés en los zapatos. Además, en el supermercado el otro día, la niña le ponía mucha atención a los zapatos de otras personas. Un sábado, la mamá llevó a la niña a la biblioteca. Ellas escogieron muchos libros acerca de los zapatos. Las dos leyeron los libros y la niña comenzó a decir palabras nuevas del tema; por ejemplo dijo "botas," "zapatillas," y "los zapatos con luces." Luego, en el dormitorio la mamá agarró diez zapatos e hicieron un juego de buscar las parejas. Luego, juntaron los zapatos de la mamá y los zapatos de la hija y los organizaron en grupos de los "zapatos grandes" y los "zapatos chiquitos."

Segunda fase: Investigar

La mamá había visto que la niña necesitaba comprar unos zapatos nuevos. Preparó para un excursión a la zapatería de Payless. En la tienda, la mamá midió el pie de su hija con el aparato de medir. Después de escoger los zapatos de tenis de princesa, la mamá enseño a su hija unos juegos de aprender. Buscaron las botas, las zapatillas, los zapatos de tenis, los zapatos con luces, y los zapatos formales. Siguiendo eso, buscaron caricaturas familiares como Elmo, Teletubbies, etc. Cuando era hora de pagar, la mamá permitió que la niña pagara el dinero al cajero. A llegar a la casa, la mamá sacó el periódico y ayudó a su hija encontrar fotos de zapatos. Luego la mamá cortó las fotos e hicieron un libro. También, la mamá coleccionó muchos zapatos de diferentes tipos y los puso en una caja para que jugara la niña independientemente.

Tercera face: Culminar

En celebración del proyecto, la mamá y la hija visitaron a la casa de la abuelita. A ella, le enseñaron el libro y los zapatos nuevos. La niña recordó muchas de las palabras nuevas en su libro. Al final, la abuelita enseño sus zapatos a la niña.

31

El proyecto del garaje
Un papá y su hijo de 4 años

Fase 1: Empezar el proyecto

Un niño de 4 años observaba mientras su papa medía el aire en las llantas y examinaba las luces de los frenos y le preguntó a su papá que hacía. El papá le enseñó a su hijo como sale el aire de la llanta. También, el papá le enseñó a su hijo como medir el aire de la llanta con el manómetro. Luego, el papá revisó las luces de los frenos y los "signal lights." Vio que su hijo estuvo muy interesado y el papá abrió la parte delantera del carro y le hizo caso a las preguntas adicionales de su hijo. El hijo preguntó, "¿Qué es?" para todas las partes del carro. El papá sacó la varilla del aceite y le enseñó a su hijo como saber si el carro necesita más aceite. Cuando entraron a la casa, el niño corrió a su mamá para decirle todo lo que había visto. La mamá agarró una pluma y papel y le explicó a su hijo que quería escribir unas de las cosas que el niño había aprendido. Mientras la mamá escribía, el papá regresó al carro y sacó la manual. Juntos, el hijo y su papá miraron a los dibujos en la manual. Durante la cena, el papá sugirió que la próxima vez que necesitará cambiar el aceite, que el hijo podría ir también. Después de la cena, el hijo y su papá hicieron una lista de 3 preguntas para el mecánico.

Fase 2: Investigación

En unos días, el papá llamó por teléfono a "Grease Spot" para ver si su hijo y él podrían observar mientras cambiaban el aceite. El papá también explicó que su hijo tenía algunas pregunta y el mecánico dijo que podrían contestarlas. El sábado siguiente, el papá y su hijo visitaron Grease Spot. El mecánico contestó las preguntas, "¿Por dónde sale el aceite viejo?" y "¿Qué significan los números en la botella de aceite?" También, el mecánico le enseñó al niño un filtro del aire. Después de su visita, el niño dibujó el garaje y los carros y los gatos. Cuando el papá pagó, agarró unos folletos que incluyeron una foto del edificio y los mecánicos. Cuando regresaron a casa, el niño jugó con sus carros de juguete y usó bloques para construir rampas. El papá se dio cuenta de lo que estaba haciendo su hijo y sugirió que pudieran construir un garaje usando una caja de cartón. El papá le preguntó a su hijo que quería incluir en su garaje e hicieron una lista de lo que dijo. Luego, le preguntó a su hijo como quería poner las partes del garaje. "¿Qué necesitas para hacer eso?" preguntó el papá. Los dos trabajaron en el proyecto de vez en cuando durante la semana. Usaron los bloques para hacer rampas para los carros y el papá cortó las puertas donde el niño indicó. El niño hizo un letrero para su garaje usando un sobre y usó "Saran Wrap" para las ventanas. Cada vez que el hijo acabó una parte del garaje, el papá refirió a la lista y le preguntó a su hijo como planeaba hacer la próxima parte. Mientras construía su edificio, el hijo seguía jugando con los carros en su garaje.

Fase 3: Culminación

Cuando acabaron la construcción del garaje, el papá le preguntó a su hijo con quien quería compartir su trabajo. El hijo decidió invitar a su primo, Joel, y su tío, Earl, a la casa para enseñarles su proyecto. Los niños jugaron por mucho tiempo con los carros. El papá escuchó a su conversación y se dio cuenta que su hijo usó muchas palabras nuevas que había aprendido en el proyecto. Antes de que salieron los invitados, Joey dijo, "Oye—¿dónde vas a lavar estos carros?" El niño miró a su papá y dijo, "¡Vamos al lavacoche!"

El proyecto de la maquina grande
Una mamá y su hijos de 4 y 6 años

Fase 1: Empezar el proyecto

Después de mover a una vecindad nueva, dos hermanos estaban muy interesados en todas las maquinas grandes que observaban trabajando alrededor de la vecindad. Todos los días observaban las maquinas e intentaban nombrarlas y describir lo que hacían. De vez en cuando, los hermanos no estaban de acuerdo y discutían. Para ayudarles no pelear tanto, su mamá sugirió que escogieran una maquina cada uno para ser "experto" sobre esa maquina. La mamá juntó unos libros sobre maquinas grandes que tenían en sus dormitorios. Cada noche, leyeron un libro y hablaron sobre cual maquina cada hermano quería estudiar. El viernes decidieron cual maquina querían estudiar; el hijo mayor escogió la excavadora y el hijo menor escogió la hormigonera. El sábado por la mañana, la mamá llevó a sus hijos a la biblioteca para buscar más recursos sobre cada maquina.

Fase 2: Investigación

Para empezar la investigación, la mamá le preguntó a sus hijos que hicieran una lista de 3 cosas que sabían sobre su maquina y 3 cosas que querían saber. Al final de la semana, la mamá y sus hijos fueron de paseo y observaron las maquinas mientras trabajaban. Cada niño tomó fotos de su maquina. Cuando un trabajador tenía un poco de tiempo, ella le preguntó si sus hijos podrían regresar el día siguiente y hacer sus preguntas. Después de revelar el rollo de fotos, la mamá ayudó a los dos niños a hacer libros simples usando las fotos. Unas fotos pegaron con las cosas que ya sabían y otras usaron para las cosas nuevas que habían aprendido. También, la mamá incluyó las maquinas en otras actividades. Para un proyecto de arte, la mamá les dio a los niños lodo para pintar como habían visto lo excavadora empujar. Les ayudó hacer impresiones de la mano usando yeso mate parecido al cemento que usaba la hormigonera. Además, ella juntó todos sus tractores de juguete y los puso en su caja de arena.

Fase 3: Culminación

Para compartir su proyecto, los niños invitaron unos amigos a la casa para una fiesta de las maquinas grandes. Enseñaron a sus amigos, los libros que habían hecho y los libros de la biblioteca. Los niños jugaron afuera en la caja de arena con los tractores e hicieron dibujos usando las rodadas de las maquinas de juguete. Los niños acabaron la fiesta con un bizcocho adornado con la ayuda de los dos hermanos con sus dos maquinas hechas de alcorza.

POWERPOINT® PRESENTATION
SETTING THE STAGE FOR LEARNING

This PowerPoint® presentation will enable you to talk with parents about how to support children's learning in the home. Read Chapter 2 to prepare for this presentation.

- Variation for Family Literacy Programs: None
- Variation for Spanish Speakers: Translate the main points.

The PowerPoint® presentation illustrates:

- Locations for project work in the home
- Materials and supplies
- Convenient storage
- Making time for project work

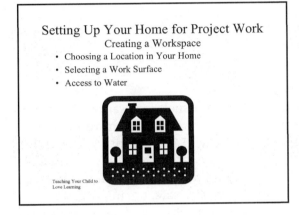

Setting Up Your Home for Project Work
Creating a Workspace
- Choosing a Location in Your Home
- Selecting a Work Surface
- Access to Water

Teaching Your Child to Love Learning

As you begin project work in your home, you will want to think of a space that will allow you to do project work. You will want an area with a table or counter for art and writing activities. You will also want the floor to be protected. Choosing a space that has water nearby is helpful when an activity calls for water, such as painting with watercolors.

Is your home ready for learning?

- How can I provide a learning environment?
- Where can I put materials needed for project work?
- How can I find time to do projects with my child?

Teaching Your Child to Love Learning

As you look at your home, you should ask yourself a few questions. Consider how you will make this work and where you can find storage for materials and for larger projects.

How can I provide a learning environment?

- Where can we work together?
- Where is it comfortable to paint, draw, and write?
- What materials do I need and where can I store them?

Teaching Your Child to Love Learning

As you look at your home, think about where you and your child can work comfortably. Like Goldilocks, you will need chairs that are not too big, not too small, but just the right size for each of you. The same is true for your work surface—table, counter, etc. You will also need to think about how the materials can be close to your work. It is frustrating when you are very engaged in work and have to stop to find scissors or glue.

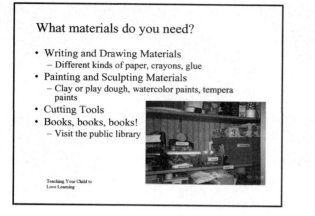

What materials do you need?

- Writing and Drawing Materials
  - Different kinds of paper, crayons, glue
- Painting and Sculpting Materials
  - Clay or play dough, watercolor paints, tempera paints
- Cutting Tools
- Books, books, books!
  - Visit the public library

Teaching Your Child to
Love Learning

When you think about materials beyond the basics, think creatively. Scissors, glue, tape, markers, paint, clay, and crayons are standards that you will need for all of your work. Beyond that, think of different kinds of paper you find in your home, boxes that can be cut up for cardboard, and kitchen utensils that can be used with clay. You will also want to remember that you will need books to support learning during your project.

How can I store the materials?
- Easy Accessibility
- Well Organized
- Home-Friendly

Teaching Your Child to
Love Learning

Storage can be a tricky issue! You want to have easy access to the materials and want them to be well organized. Children need to be responsible for materials and put them away neatly when they are finished. Plastic tubs and rolling carts are small, fairly inexpensive ways to keep materials safe, organized, and out of the hands of younger brothers and sisters. They can also be stored easily in the home in places such as a closet or the garage.

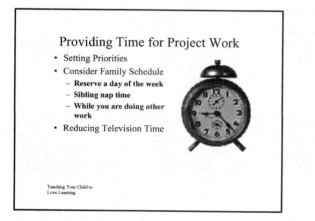

Providing Time for Project Work
- Setting Priorities
- Consider Family Schedule
  - **Reserve a day of the week**
  - **Sibling nap time**
  - **While you are doing other work**
- Reducing Television Time

Teaching Your Child to
Love Learning

Time is an issue for many busy families. To make time for project work, the project has to be viewed as an important time for your child during their day. Each family needs to think about when project work would most easily fit in to their schedule. Families also need to think about turning off the television, which helps make time for project work.

POWERPOINT® PRESENTATION
FEATURED PROJECT—
MAUDE, THE DOG PROJECT
3-YEAR-OLD BOY AND HIS FAMILY

Read the Maude the Dog Project, pages 17–19 in *Teaching Your Child to Love Learning*, to prepare to share this PowerPoint® presentation.

- Variation for Family Literacy Programs: This presentation is made from a family history book and may be printed as a book.

This project illustrates:

- Home environment for project work
- Project focused on a family pet
- Father involved in a project
- Incorporation of surveying, tallying, and graphing
- Construction of a model

The project was completed by Gordon Swenor with the help of his parents. The topic was their dog, Maude.

In the book, we talk about setting up a place to do project work. This does not have to be a separate place used only for project work. Gordon and his dad worked at their kitchen table and on the floor. Since Gordon's Dad is a big man, child-sized furniture would not be comfortable for him.

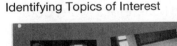

At first the Swenors thought they might study dinosaurs because that was the only thing they could remember that 3-year-old Gordon talked about. However, when they observed Gordon and looked for what he was truly interested in and cared about, they saw how much Gordon loved his dog. Here he is playing with Maude on the couch. He even built a Lego model of Maude.

First drawing of Maude
January 14, 2003

When they began the project, they sat down with paper, and everyone drew a picture of Maude. Here is Gordon's first drawing. He drew a body, legs, and a head.

Investigating during field-site visit

Gordon went with Maude to the vet's for his checkup. (Read Gordon's Words). Gordon is noticing things in the examining room. He is also describing the examining room as he sees it. Looking at photos of field-site visits and having your child tell you about the picture is a good way to see what your child has learned, what words he is using, and what he finds interesting.

Investigating by interviewing an expert.

Gordon was very curious about the little triangle shape pad at the back of each of Maude's feet. He thought it might honk if you squeezed it. He saw the similarity between the shape and a horn. He found out it was the accessory pad and did not honk.

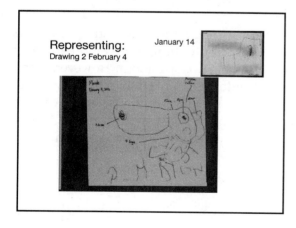

Representing:
Drawing 2 February 4   January 14

After they had studied Maude for a while, Gordon made a new picture of Maude. The picture up in the corner is his picture that he had drawn almost three weeks earlier. (Point out the parts of the drawing and the labels on the screen. Ask participants to describe the differences that they see. What has Gordon learned?)

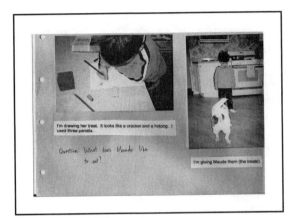

Supporting development: Tally chart of parts of Maude's body

Gordon's mother Mimi taught tallying to Gordon. She made a chart so that he could tally Maude's body parts. This is a good example of a parent recognizing a child's interest and teaching the child skills. Because the child was interested in counting how many parts Maude had (dogs have four legs while people only have two), she went the next step and showed him how to record what he was learning. This also shows children the value of such things as numbers and words.

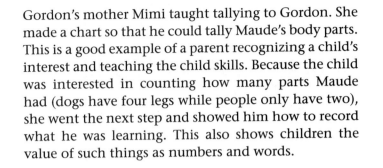

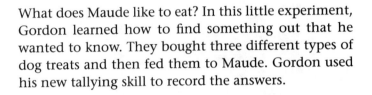

What does Maude like to eat? In this little experiment, Gordon learned how to find something out that he wanted to know. They bought three different types of dog treats and then fed them to Maude. Gordon used his new tallying skill to record the answers.

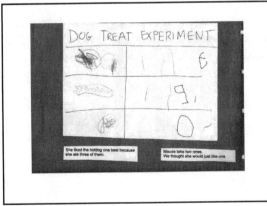

Here is the tally sheet from the Dog Treat Experiment. What do you think Gordon learned from this experience?

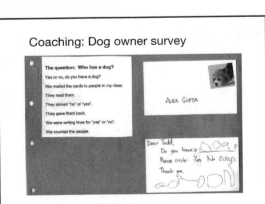

Coaching: Dog owner survey

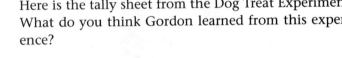

This is an example of coaching a child to do something when he is not ready to do the skill. Mimi and Gordon were talking about which of Gordon's school friends had a dog. Gordon wanted to know so Mimi said they could do a survey. In the preschool each child had a mailbox. They thought they could send a card to each child to complete with parent help. Mimi made a card leaving space for Gordon to sign it and write "dog." This was a lot to expect a 3-year-old to do 20 times! She decided it would have been better if she prepared all of the cards herself.

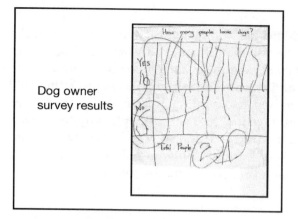

Dog owner survey results

Gordon did enjoy the tallying of the survey results. There were a lot of dog owners in Gordon's class.

Maude and Blue's Clues

Gordon was interested in Blue's Clues, a television program with a dog that has a paw print as a logo. He wondered if Maude's paw print would be the same. This lead to a fun activity in which they made a print of Maude's paw but also Gordon's foot.

Making Maude

Gordon and his dad made this dog together out of newspapers, cardboard, and glue. Joel, the father, did a lot of the building, which he enjoyed. Gordon did most of the painting. While they were doing it, they talked about Maude. It was a fun time for both of them.

Celebrating Event: Maude goes to school.

To celebrate the end of the project, Maude came to visit the classroom. Maude was quite a hit in the pre-school.

UNIT 2

Selecting a Topic and Beginning Investigation

TALK
What Makes a Good Project Topic?

Directions for Facilitators

This should be an informal talk by the facilitator. The main point is that some topics make good projects and others do not. There are many things that children are interested in learning about. Children can learn by talking about something, listening to a book about it, observing it, etc. However, in project work we are looking for a topic that is worth studying over a period of time and that holds a great deal of interest for children. Share your own ideas about what might be a good topic within your neighborhood or city.

Prepare for the talk by reading Chapter 4 in *Teaching Your Child to Love Learning*.

Main Points for Talk

The Main Points to be made in this talk are summarized on page 6 of the Family Project Planning Journal. Have participants look at this page as you discuss it.

Variation for Family Literacy Programs

Use the handout on the next page instead of referring to the pages in the book or the journal.

Variation for Spanish Speakers

Facilitators should refer to page 6 in Spanish version of the Family Project Planning Journal.

What Makes a Good Project Topic?

1. A good project topic has real objects. Children enjoy touching, moving, and using real objects in their play.

2. A good project topic is something your child knows something about.

3. A good project topic can be investigated at a place you can visit again and again.

4. A good project topic can be researched by your child.

5. A good project topic enables your child to use skills and methods appropriate for his age.

6. A good project topic is worth studying.

7. A good project topic is related to your child's world.

ACTIVITY
Choosing the Best Topic

Directions for Facilitators

This activity will give parents an opportunity to think about appropriate topics for project work. It follows the talk on topic selection.

1. Pass out the handout "Choosing the Best Topic." You may have one copy per parent, or if you want more interaction between parents, you can have one copy for two or three parents. You may also do this activity as a whole group if parents are hesitant to read.
2. Tell the parents: "We are going to look at these topics in pairs. Compare the two topics that are side by side. Which of these would be better as a topic for a project? Remember that there really is no correct answer." For example, a project on corn would be great if you lived in a rural area of the Midwest, but what if you lived in Chicago? "Think about a project for our children here in _____. We will do the first one as a whole group. Thinking about *cats* and *giraffes*. Which would be best for our children here?" "Why?" The discussion might include: "Where could we see a real giraffe?" "If your child is allergic to cats, you might not want to do cats."
3. Have the parents talk about the rest of the list circling the one best choice. Remember that there are really no right answers.

Follow-Up

Call out the choices, and see which item each group selected. Some comments you might want to make include:

Cats vs. Giraffes—Cats is probably better because it is difficult to see a real giraffe except in very large zoos. However, if there is a giraffe in a zoo near you, this could be a good topic. Cats are also better if the child has access to a cat to study frequently, which is one of the characteristics of a good project.

Pizza Hut® vs. Stores—Pizza Hut® is a better topic because it is real and concrete; stores is usually too broad as a topic. It is better to study a particular store or restaurant (say Pizza Hut® rather than pizza restaurants) because the child can picture this one restaurant and think deeply about what he or she knows about it.

History of Thanksgiving vs. Cooking Thanksgiving Dinner—Thanksgiving is a historical topic that is not good because young children are confused by time. Historical topics do not generally make good topics for children younger than seven. It is also not concrete. However, cooking Thanksgiving dinner is about concrete items and involves many skills.

Combines (or harvesters) vs. Sailboats—Both of these topics are good if they are part of the child's environment. If the families live in a rural area and see crops harvested, then combines is a good topic. If they live near the sea, a lake, or a river where sailboats can be observed, then this is a good topic. If neither of these are part of the lives of the children and families, then neither are good topics for projects.

Cars vs. Semitrailer trucks—The choice will totally depend on the group and the family. If father is a truck driver, it would be a wonderful topic. The availability of field-sites and experts will be the determining factor.

Ocean vs. River—Another topic that depends on the availability of field-sites and experts. The point we want to make is that topics are better if they are easily accessible and in the locality of the family. This is a good time to talk about how a child could study the ocean if there isn't one near by. They would have to use books, videos, and talk to other people who have seen the ocean. This is *second-hand (or passive) learning*. To accomplish our goals of independence and confidence for our children, they need *first-hand (hands-on or active) learning*.

City Council vs. Street Repair—Rarely will city council win out! This is very abstract for children and hard to study. Maybe if a child has a father who is a council member this could work—even then we would recommend that they study City Hall!

Road Construction vs. Dam Construction—Most construction sites are very interesting to children and regular observation of construction of anything going up nearby can be a wonderful project for the whole family. Again, the closeness of the site for repeat visits and access to experts is important.

Archaeology vs. Rocks—Archaeology is historical so this would not be as good a topic for children younger than seven. A project on rocks provides many opportunities for hands-on learning. Then again, archaeology can be very hands-on, and if there is a site nearby, this could be a good project. We would refocus the topic to be excavation of a site.

Weather vs. What Makes Snow—Weather is abstract and very broad. Snow can be touched, smelled, manipulated (rolled, piled, and melted). However if one lives in Arizona, snow would not be a good topic. Even in Arizona, however, weather is difficult to narrow to a topic young children can study in depth. Children who are older than six, however, can remember weather from season to season and day to day. Children this age are also able to read, measure, and use data charts so the broader topic of weather might work for them.

Cooking vs. Making Bread—Making bread is a better topic because it is narrow enough to provide a good focus. A child could do a project on bread, complete it, and then do another project on some other food. This would be better than a broad topic that is difficult to define.

Bicycles vs. Religion—Again the concrete, easily accessible topic wins. Religion is too abstract for a project for young children. This is a good time to talk about the idea that there are many things that we teach our children in other ways—through conversation, modeling, or direct instruction. Just because a topic is not a good *project* doesn't mean it isn't a good thing to teach young children.

Variation

Facilitators may wish to change the items to match their community and the experiences of the families.

Variation for Family Literacy Programs

You may change choices to match the literacy level of your group, let volunteers read the items, or do this activity as a whole group reading the items yourself if parents are hesitant to read.

Variation for Spanish Speakers

The handout with the list of choices is provided in Spanish on page 45. Note that a few of the choices have been changed to be more culturally relevant.

Choosing the Best Topic

Look at each pair of topics. Which topic do you think would be the best topic for project work for children in our area? For example, which is the better topic: Cats or giraffes? Choose one topic from each pair, circle it, and then talk about why you selected it.

Cats	Giraffes
Pizza Hut®	Stores
Origin of Thanksgiving	Cooking a Thanksgiving Dinner
Combines or Harvesters	Sailboats
Cars	Semi-Trucks
The Ocean	The River
City Council	Street Repair
Road Construction	Dam Construction
Archaeology	Rocks
Weather	What Makes Snow
Cooking	Baking Bread
Bicycles	Religion

Escogiendo el mejor tema

Lee los do temas. ¿Cuál tema será mejor para un proyecto con los niños que viven en nuestra área? Por ejemplo, ¿Cuál es el mejor para que los niños estudien—los gatos o las jirafas?

Los gatos	Las jirafas
Pizza Hut®	Las tiendas
Origen del 16 de septiembre	Como hacer mole
Los tractores/las cosechadoras	Los barcos
Los carros	Los camiones
El océano	El río
El consejo municipal	La reparación de las calles
La construcción de las autopistas	La construcción de una presa
Arqueología	Piedras/Rocas
El clima	Que hace la nieve
Cocinar	Como concinar el pan
Los carros	La religíon

ACTIVITY
Reporting on Children's Interests

Directions for Facilitators

Individually the parents can share observations of their children since the last meeting, telling what they wrote on page 4 of the Family Project Planning Journal.

- What interested the children?
- How did they know the children were interested?
- Is this a possible topic for a project?

Encourage parents to share what they have observed and talk about possible project topics. This is a valuable opportunity for everyone to think about observing children and to apply the guidelines for topic selection. It is helpful to ask parents to share just a few sentences about each of these questions. It might also be helpful to put the questions on an overhead or on chart paper on the wall to keep the conversation focused.

Fewer than 10 Participants

If you have 10 or fewer participants, this sharing of interests and topic possibilities can occur in a whole group with the facilitator recording ideas on a wall chart. Sharing with the whole group might also be helpful for parents who need or want more guidance. The facilitator will want to transfer the information to the documentation list later. If you have more than one facilitator, each facilitator can take a group.

More than 10 Participants

Groups larger than 10 can be subdivided into small groups of no more than five. Have each group write the topics from their group on a wall chart for everyone to see. When the group comes back together, a member of the group can share the list.

Variation for Family Literacy Programs

This discussion requires no adaptation.

Variation for Spanish Speakers

Use the Spanish version of the Family Project Planning Journal.

ACTIVITY
Using a Web to Find Out What Children Know

Materials

- Large chart paper and different colors of markers
- Examples of topic webs

Directions for Facilitators

This activity will give parents some experience making a web so they can do this activity with their children. Read pages 56–57 of *Teaching Your Child to Love Learning* in preparation for this activity. You may also want to mark in your book the following pages that show webs so you can share them with your group:

- Cooking web, page 42
- Caterpillar web, page 46
- Horses web, page 57
- Race car web, page 61

1. In a large group, choose an appropriate project topic, like shoes or bread. Ask the group to tell you what they think their child might know about the topic. Make a web on large paper as they give you ideas.
2. Break into small groups, and give each group a piece of chart paper and markers. Encourage each group to choose a topic of interest in one of their families and make a web of what they think the children might know.
3. Ask each small group to share their topic web with the large group and tape them up for display on a wall.
4. Provide time for questions, and ask the group which topics were easier to web.
5. Talk about ways they might ask children what they know.
6. Explain that they can add to the web using a different color of marker as children learn more about the topic.

Variations

You may wish to have each family web the topic of their own children.

Divide the group into pairs. Have one member of each pair pretend to be the parent and the other a child, and have them make a web together. Your group might enjoy doing this as adults and choosing a topic about which they might not have a lot of knowledge, for example, the solar system.

Assign the group to make a web of a topic with their children and bring it to the next meeting.

Variation for Family Literacy Programs

Webbing is an excellent vocabulary builder and can be integrated into other parent and child activities.

Variation for Spanish Speakers

Webbing example should be done in Spanish.

POWERPOINT® PRESENTATION

FEATURED PROJECT—THE RACE CAR PROJECT 4-YEAR-OLD BOY AND HIS FAMILY

Read the Race Car Project, pages 59–63 in *Teaching Your Children to Love Learning.* Emphasize the genuine interest of the child in the topic and the mother's ability to pickup on that and learn with the child.

This project illustrates:
- A topic of consistent interest
- A mother's involvement in a child's interest
- A field-site visit
- Webbing
- Celebrating by making a poster

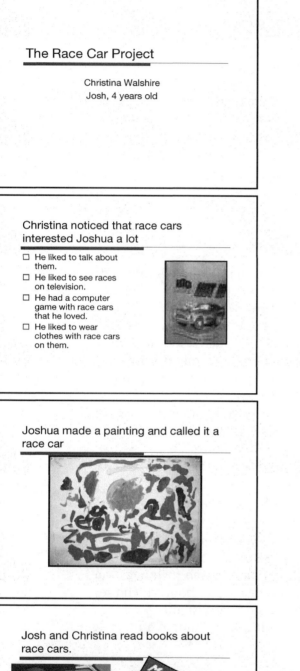

Joshua had an interest in race cars for some time before this project began. Christina noted that Josh's interest started very early and had been consistent. She had not thought about sharing this interest with Joshua until she learned about projects.

Joshua made this painting at home. He called his painting a race car.

Books about topics are usually easy to find. Some books like these are written for Joshua's age; however, books that are also for older children and adults can be helpful if they have photos or diagrams in them.

Joshua had questions about race cars.

☐ How do they build the engine of a race car?

☐ Do you put oil in your car while you are in the pit?

☐ How much gas do you put in your car before the race?

☐ What is your number?

☐ Do you use a jack under your car?

Finding out what your child wants to know about a topic is an important part of project work. It provides a focus for investigation and helps you understand the level of understanding your child has about the topic.

Josh's first drawing of a race car

Josh recognized race cars but his first drawing showed he was not too sure about the parts.

He did write letters for gas where he thought the gas tank would be

This is a good example of a 4-year-old's first attempts at drawing. Christina wisely accepted the drawing and wrote down what Joshua said about it.

Christina was able to find someone who had a real race car to be an expert.

☐ Joshua was able to sit in the race car and pretend

☐ This is a prized picture on Joshua's poster!

Finding an expert and a place to visit is sometimes a challenge in project work, but it has a big payoff in excitement and interest of both children and adults.

Joshua recorded the answers to the questions

☐ How do they build the engine of a race car? *A mechanic builds it.*

☐ Do you put oil in your car while you are in the pit? *Not in the pit.*

☐ How much gas do you put in your car before the race? *We don't use gas, we use an alcohol fuel cell. It takes 22 gallons.*

☐ What is your number? *18.*

☐ Do you use a jack under your car? *Yes.*

It is important to go back and revisit the questions that your child has and record the answers. This helps your child see that they can find answers to questions and that their thoughts are respected.

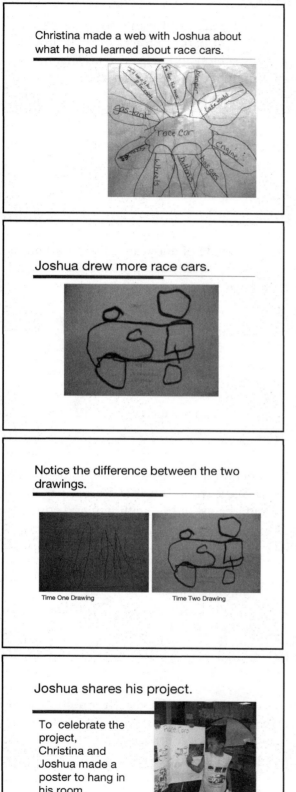

Christina made a web with Joshua about what he had learned about race cars.

Joshua drew more race cars.

Notice the difference between the two drawings.

Time One Drawing

Time Two Drawing

Joshua shares his project.

To celebrate the project, Christina and Joshua made a poster to hang in his room.

A web is like a list of what a child knows but is organized like a drawing. Making a web of what a child knows about a topic helps the adult provide experiences that are appropriate. If additions to the web are made with a different color of marker, everyone can see what the child is learning. Lists of words that a child has learned are also very helpful.

This is Joshua's second drawing of a race car after he had an opportunity and encouragement to seriously study race cars.

When two drawings or other pieces of work that have been done over a period of time are collected, they are often referred to as Time One, Time Two, etc. They show the child focusing on the same subject. What differences are there between the two drawings? What do they show about changes in understanding?

Taking time to gather children's work, display it, and share it with others helps build a child's confidence as a learner. It provides an opportunity for adults to have discussions about topics of interest to the child and to have meaningful positive interactions with the child.

POWERPOINT® PRESENTATION

INTRODUCTION TO INVESTIGATION AND REPRESENTATION

Read Chapter 5 in *Teaching Your Child to Love Learning*. This is an introduction to possible ways of representing. As a follow-up to the presentation, you may choose to review and discuss pages 12–15 of the Family Project Planning Journal.

This PowerPoint® presentation introduces:

- Field-site visits
- Choosing experts
- Representation
- Drawing
- Play as representation

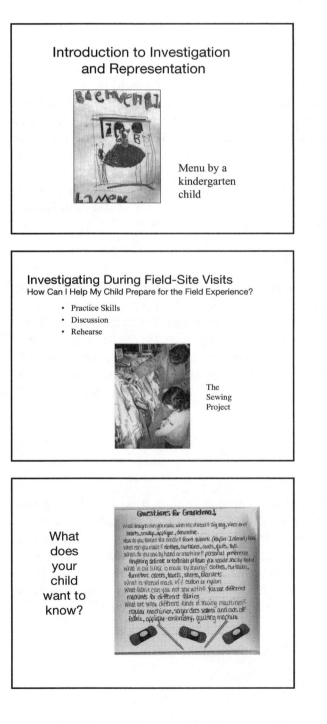

Field-site visits provide many opportunities to investigate and build confidence as a learner. It helps if you take time practicing some of the skills with your child before the day of the field-site visit. For example, you can sketch items around the house using the clipboard. It is also helpful to talk about what questions your child wants to have answered and even to practice asking them.

Making up questions and then writing them down provides practice in many school skills, including the use of writing, how print carries meaning, and letter and word recognition.

Include Experts in the Investigations

- What skills will the expert be able to share?
- Do they have real objects they could lend your child?
- Do they have time to spend with your family?

The Horse Project

Young children process their learning by representation.

- Drawings and Sketches
- Paintings
- Constructions

The Shoe Project

Even very young children will draw

- Here are Amy's drawings about bats

Often representation takes the form of play environments

It is helpful to think about, in advance, what you will want an expert to do with your child. These are good questions to ask before you contact someone to help with your project. It is more important that an expert be positive and flexible with your child than that they have a wealth of knowledge about the topic. They merely need to know more than your child does about the topic. An uncle with a new pick-up truck may be a better "expert" on trucks for your child than an auto mechanic.

Think about items that your child might draw or sketch. Is there something that would be a good subject of a painting? Remember that it is difficult for young children to draw big objects like houses. It is much easier for them to draw a smaller item or even a part of an item. Drawing toy models, such as a toy race car, is another way to make it easier for your child. As you work with your child and the item, be sure to use words about the parts and the uses of the item so you can help your child build vocabulary.

Don't underestimate the ability of your child to draw. This drawing is by a 3-year-old. Very young children will begin to draw if encouraged. You can model drawing. Remember drawing is an excellent way for children to study. Never tell a child, "I never could draw!" Drawing should be something all children can do. They will get better with practice and so will you.

Young children often represent their learning by creation of play things such as this bat cave for Aimee's toy bat. Children will also create play environments, such as arranging furniture or making accessories to make a hospital or a pizza restaurant. As they play, they will assume roles and use words that show how much they have learned about the place.

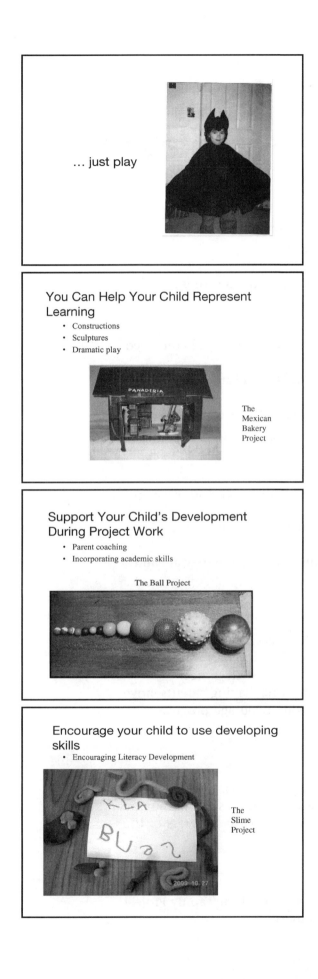

... just play

You Can Help Your Child Represent Learning
- Constructions
- Sculptures
- Dramatic play

The Mexican Bakery Project

Support Your Child's Development During Project Work
- Parent coaching
- Incorporating academic skills

The Ball Project

Encourage your child to use developing skills
- Encouraging Literacy Development

The Slime Project

Pretending is a good way for children to incorporate what they are learning and to think about what they have learned. Pretend play extends well into the elementary and middle school years.

Don't hesitate to join in the fun with your child. You can help create play things. This Mexican Bakery was created with the help of the parents and became a wonderful shared experience. Feel free to work with your child and even join in the pretend play.

There are many opportunities for you to help your child learn skills during project work. Unlike school experiences that are focused on typical development of children of that age, project work at home can exactly match your child's developmental level. If they are interested and able to do things beyond your expectations, use projects as an opportunity to support that. This sequence activity was done by toddlers. If there are areas that are challenging for your child, project work is a good opportunity to practice these skills at home.

Project work is a wonderful opportunity for children to become involved in reading and writing. This sign that says "clay bugs" is an example of how a preschool child was motivated to try writing.

Unit 3

Investigation and Representation

ACTIVITY
What Phase Are You In?

This is a good activity to do as parents are entering the meeting room.

Materials

- Copies of the next pages of the Project Flowchart enlarged and taped end to end to make a continuous line
- Stickers or small Post-It® arrows for families to indicate where they are in their project
- (Facilitators may want to laminate the enlarged flow chart to use with other groups)

Directions for Facilitators

1. As parents enter, welcome them and give them a sticker to place on the flowchart.
2. Parents put stickers on the flowchart to indicate where they are in the progress of their project.
3. As the group settles down, let each family show where they are and tell what they have done up to this time.

Variations

Instead of enlarging the flowchart by photocopying, make an overhead of the flowchart that shows all the phases. Project the flowchart onto a blank wall, and let parents put post-it notes where they are in their project.

You may want to use this flowchart at each meeting, having parents move their markers when they join the group. This will encourage progress with your group.

Variation for Family Literacy Programs

Use the flowchart handout for family literacy programs. Have copies in journals, and have participants mark on the copy the date instead of moving a marker, then have them write in their journals about the progress of the project each time they make a new mark.

Variation for Spanish Speakers

Use the flow chart on page 3 of the Spanish version of the Family Project Planning Journal to prepare materials for this activity.

Phase One

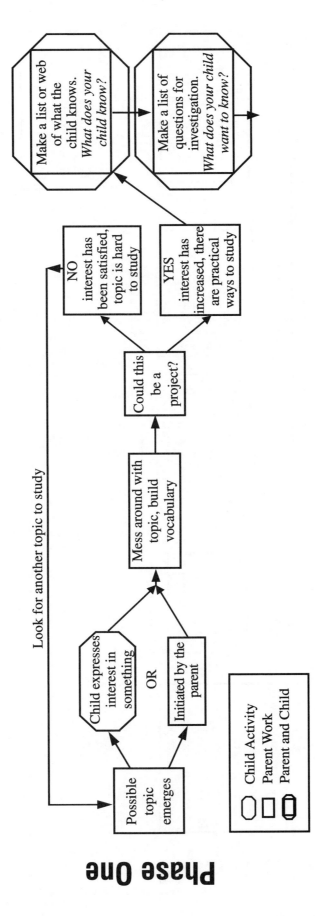

Make a list or web of what the child knows. *What does your child know?*

Make a list of questions for investigation. *What does your child want to know?*

NO interest has been satisfied, topic is hard to study

YES interest has increased, there are practical ways to study

Could this be a project?

Mess around with topic, build vocabulary

Look for another topic to study

Child expresses interest in something

OR

Initiated by the parent

Possible topic emerges

Child Activity
Parent Work
Parent and Child

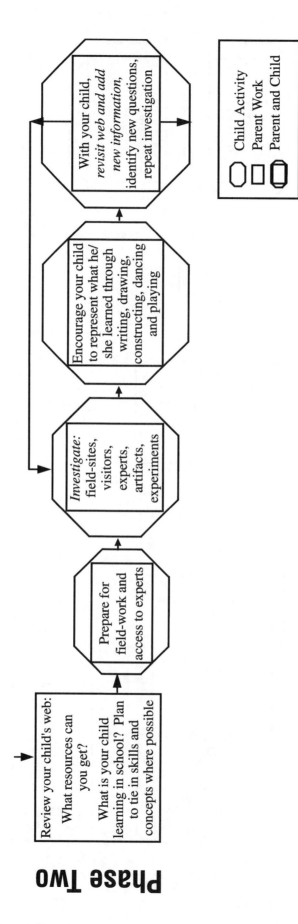

Phase Two

Review your child's web: What resources can you get?

What is your child learning in school? Plan to tie in skills and concepts where possible

Prepare for field-work and access to experts

Investigate: field-sites, visitors, experts, artifacts, experiments

Encourage your child to represent what he/she learned through writing, drawing, constructing, dancing and playing

With your child, *revisit web and add new information,* identify new questions, repeat investigation

Child Activity

Parent Work

Parent and Child

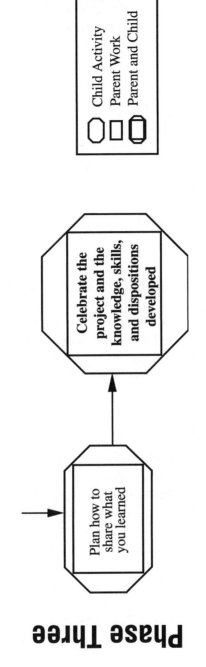

Phase Three

Plan how to share what you learned

Celebrate the project and the knowledge, skills, and dispositions developed

○ Child Activity
□ Parent Work
▯ Parent and Child

ACTIVITY
Sketching Keys

Materials

- Paper and pencil for drawing
- Each participant's keys

Directions for Facilitators

The purpose of this activity is to have parents discover the power of drawing as a way of studying. As you discuss this activity, talk about drawing as the way that a child can take notes. Stress that this activity is not a test of drawing ability!

1. Ask parents to think about their keys without removing them and looking at them.
2. Ask them to make a sketch of what they think they look like.
3. Next ask them to get out their keys, put them in front of them, and sketch them again.
4. Tell parents to share their sketches with someone near them.

Ask these questions:

1. Were your drawings different?
2. Did you learn anything about your keys that you didn't know?
3. What things did you see that you were not aware of?
4. How is drawing like studying?
5. How can drawing help your children?

No Variations Needed

ACTIVITY
Representation Experience for Parents

Materials

- A variety of art media such as wire, clay, paints, collage materials, and any other materials that are available.
- Tools such as scissors, glue, and markers
- An item of interest such as a tool, basket, plant, etc. The more detail (color, texture, etc) the item has, the better.

Directions for Facilitators

The purpose of this activity is to provide parents with an experience using art media, to help them feel comfortable with creative activities and to see how many different ways children can represent their learning.

1. Have the group agree on one item that they will all represent.
2. Place the item so all parents can observe it closely at times but also view it throughout the activity.
3. Tell parents they may choose how they want to represent it, but all different ways must be modeled. First come, first served on the choice of materials
4. Have parents use the art materials provided to represent what they have observed. If they complete one representation before the time is up, they can try another medium.

Use the following questions to focus discussion after the activity:

1. Is it helpful to have the item in front of you?
2. How would your work have changed if the item had not been in front of you?
3. Would you be interested in trying to do the activity again with a different type of art material?
4. Do you think your work would improve if you were given an opportunity to try again?
5. Would it have been helpful to work with a partner who could provide you with ideas and feedback?
6. Did you have enough time to do your best work?
7. Is having all the materials ready for you helpful in the creative process?
8. Were you physically comfortable so you could concentrate on your work instead of the physical environment?
9. Is it interesting to you that people were representing the same item and yet they look so different?

Finish the session by reminding parents that the feelings they had about the activity are similar to those children will have. For example, children need access to materials, time to do their work, and a comfortable environment. This activity should help parents experience project work from the child's point of view.

TALK
Stages of Representation

Directions for Facilitators

Review the charts on development and coaching in Chapter 8 of *Teaching Your Child to Love Learning*:

Representation Through Play, page 123
Representation Through Art, page 124
Learning to Write, page 125
Learning to Read, page 128
Learning to Think Mathematically, page 131

If your participants do not have the book, then make copies of the charts to share with them. Look through each chart and talk about:

1. The natural progress of skills
2. The way we can assist children by helping or coaching them to the next level
3. How expecting children to jump ahead and do skills at a much higher level is unreasonable, and the need to allow children time to develop skills
4. How we can celebrate children's growth by observing their progress

Variations

The concepts in this section of *Teaching Your Child to Love Learning* are especially meaningful for most parents and are likely to have an impact on how they respond to their child's efforts. Facilitators are encouraged to look for examples meaningful to their group and to refer back to these pages as projects progress. For parents who are reading the book, simply drawing attention to the charts and discussing them briefly will be adequate; for other parents it may be helpful to spread this activity out over several sessions.

Variation for Family Literacy Programs

Each chart could be a topic of study for a week with observations and journaling coordinated with the reading of the charts.

Variation for Spanish Speakers

Translations and adaptations of the charts are provided on the following pages.

REPRESENTACIÓN POR EL JUEGO

Representación por . . .	Como es	El progreso típico
El juego imitativo	El niño juega con los objetos reales. Empieza a los 12 meses y sigue durante la escuela primaria.	Primero, usan objetos verdaderos para pretender. Después substituyen otro objeto y al fin pueden pretender sin ningún objeto. El juego no dura por más de unos minutos.
El juego de pretender	Empieza con el niño pequeño jugando con los objetos y haciendo sonidos mientras juega. A los 3 y 4 años, se pone la ropa y juega a "ser" una persona por ejemplo la mamá.	Imita sin palabras. Después usa palabras y habla como la persona que representa. En general, el juego dura por menos de 10 minutos.
El juego socio-dramático	A los 4 y 5 años, los niños escogen a ser una persona, y los "guiones" son más elaborados.	Se distingue de las etapas anteriores porque requiere la interacción verbal. Exige planificación de cómo hablar, vestirse, y actuar en el papel. El juego dure por más de 10 minutos.

Information from: *Pathways to Play: Developing Play Skills in Young Children* by Sandra Heidemann and Deborah Hewitt, Readleaf Press (June 1992); *The Creative Curriculum for Preschool* by Diane Trister Dodge, Laura J. Colker, Cate Heroman, and Toni S. Bickart; Teaching Strategies, 4th edition (June 2002); *The Effects of Sociodramatic Play on Disadvantaged Preschool Children* by Sara Smilansky, Wiley, (1968).

REPRESENTACIONES POR EL ARTE

Representaciones por . . .	A que aparece	El progreso típico
Garabatos desorganizados	Garabatos hechos al azar.	Típico para niños de 2 años. Fingen como si estuvieran dibujando en la misma manera que se finge leer por abrir el libro y hacen como si lee.
Garabatos controlados	Los garabatos tienen forma y dirección.	Típico para niños de 2 años y algunos de 3 años. Otra vez, el proceso de dibujar o pintar es lo que es importante; el dibujo no va a ser una representación realista.
Nombrar un dibujo que no planearon	Los niños hacen líneas o formas y luego relata lo que dibujaron a sus intereses.	Muchos niños de 3 años dibujan y luego relatan su dibujo al tema del proyecto.
Dibujar	El dibujo es planeado y hecho por mirar al objeto o dibujar el objeto de memoria. Los productos son reconocible.	A los 4 años, los niños conocen sus habilidades de crear imágenes que relatan a lo que estudian. Siguen mejorando sus habilidades de dibujar durante los años en la escuela primaria.

LOS NIVELES DE ESCRITURA

Escribir de garabatos	*(garabatos escritos a mano)*
Escribir de formas que son parecidas a letras	UXLO(mm)
Escribir las letras al azar	T BRSCL
Escribir con las vocales	Ao i o (Amo mi osito.)
Escribir de una manera fonética	prdI mI dItE. (Perdí mi diente.)
Escritura tradicional	Quiero una galleta.

NIVELES DE LECTURA

Reconocer letras en su ambiente	Su hijo(a) mira la M grande en los "arcos amarillos" y grita, "¡Dice McDonald's!"
Hacer una asociación entre el lenguaje oral y el lenguaje escrito	Su hijo(a) empieza entender que las palabras que ve en los libros son las que escucha cuando Ud. lo lee un cuento.
Reconocer la primera letra en su nombre	Su hijo(a) indentifica y grita cada vez que ve la letra que empieza su nombre. "¡Mira! McDonald's tiene la letra M como mi nombre Miguel!"
Reconocer su nombre y los nombres de sus amigos	Su hijo(a) empieza a reconocer su propio nombre y los nombres de todos sus amigos.
Hacer una asociación con los sonidos y las letras	Su hijo(a) empieza a escuchar los sonidos que hacen las letras y a decir cosas como, "La letra F dice FFFFF."
Escuchar e identificar palabras que riman	Su hijo(a) empieza a interrumpir cuando estás leyendo y dice, "Oye—¡mesa y fresa suenan al mismo!"
Reconocer palabras conocidos fuera del contexto	Su hijo(a) empieza a reconocer palabras que escucha a menudo, por ejemplo: mamá, papá, no, es, sí, mi, tu, y, yo. Se llaman palabras de frecuencia.
Intentar reconocer los sonidos o sílabas en palabras	Su hijo(a) empieza a reconocer los sonidos y las sílabas mientras usa las ilustraciones para adivinar lo que quiere decir el texto.
Leer con más fluidez	Cuando su hijo(a) empieza a leer, va a querer leer los mismos libros una y otra vez, aumentando su fluidez y su confianza en su habilidad de leer.

TRANSLATION OF LEARNING TO THINK MATHEMATICALLY, PAGE 131, TEACHING YOUR CHILD TO LOVE LEARNING

NIVELES DE DESTREZAS MATEMÁTICAS

Destreza matemática	Descripción	Progreso típico
Clasificar	Organizar y agrupar objetos por el color, la forma, el tamaño, el uso etc.	Niños de 2 años pueden clasificar por el color (por ejemplo: pader clasificar los dulces M & M's por el color) Niños de 3 a 4 años pueden clasificar por el color, el tamaño, y la forma (por ejemplo: pader clasificar bloques) Niños de los 5 años y más pueden clasificar por el uso, o categorías como animales del zoológico o animales del rancho
Hacer patrones y diseños	Reconocer, copiar e inventar un patrón	Niños de 4 años pueden reconocer un patrón (por ejemplo: niño/ niña, niño, niña en la fila) Niños de 4 a 5 años pueden copiar un patrón (por ejemplo: los colores de las cuentas cuando hacen un collar) En el kindergarten, los niños ya empiezan inventar o hacer sus propios patrones y diseños
El concepto de los números	Demostrar interés en los números y contar	Niños de 3 años pueden emparejar el número con artículos (por ejemplo: un plato para cada miembro de la familia) Niños de 3 a 4 años pueden contar con entendimiento hasta cinco artículos En el kindergarten, los niños pueden contar con entendimiento hasta 20 y saber que unos números indican más y otros menos Niños en la escuela primaria pueden usar los números para resolver problemas matemáticos
Geometría	Identificar y nombrar muchas formas	Niños de 3 años pueden emparejar algunas formas Niños de 4 años pueden identificar las formas y nombrarlas Niños de 5 años pueden hacer formas Niños en la primaria pueden resolver problemas y rompecabezas usando las formas
Medir	Medir	Niños de 3 a 4 años usan palabras para comparar (por ejemplo: grande/ pequeño, largo, corto) Niños de 4 años empiezan a usar maneras que no son normalizados para medir (por ejemplo: medir un objeto usando bloques, o usando las balanzas para balancear) Niños de kindergarten empiezan a usar herramientas normalizadas para medir (por ejemplo: la regla, una balanza con números, etc.) Niños en la primaria empiezan a usar herramientas más complicadas para resolver problemas (por ejemplo: el metro, balanzas con números)
Tiempo	Desarrollar su concepto del tiempo y la hora	Niños de 3 años desarrollan su concepto de hoy, mañana, el pasado y el futuro Niños de 4 años empiezan a emparejar un significado a días específicos (por ejemplo: los domingos voy a la iglesia) Niños de kindergarten empiezan a entender los días de la semana y los meses Niños en la primaria entienden el concepto de un año, las temporadas y eventos históricos que ocurrieron hace muchos años

This information is summarized from *The Omnibus Guidelines: Preschool Through Third Grade* by Judy R. Jablon, Dorothea B. Marsden, Samuel J. Meisels, and Margo Dichtelmiller, Rebus and Associates (1994)

TALK
Principles of Coaching

Directions for Facilitators

During the review of the charts on the development of representation skills, or soon after, it is helpful to have a talk on coaching, which is described in Chapter 8. If your participants do not have the book, then make copies of the handout on the next page to share with them. A good place to start on the topic of coaching is the general principles of coaching.

Be sure in your talk on coaching to make the following points:

1. What does and does not make effective coaching.
2. The principles of coaching presented on page 117 and on the handout on the next page
3. If you haven't discussed the difference between encouragement and praise yet from Chapter 7, do it here.

Variation for Spanish Speakers

The handout on the principles of coaching is provided in Spanish on page 70.

Principles of Coaching Children

1. Your child will develop skill at a pace similar to other children but with her own individuality. It is important to be flexible in expectations.

2. Not all skills are appropriate to teach; your child must be ready for the skill physically and mentally. For example, trying to teach a 2-year-old to read is not productive when in a few years it can be accomplished easily.

3. Most skills are learned step-by-step, with each skill building a foundation for the next skill.

4. You can support your child's acquisition of skills and their development by providing motivation and opportunities to practice.

Los principios de como ayudar a su hijo aprender

1. Su hijo desarrolla a un paso semejante a los otros niños pero lo hace a su propio ritmo. Es importante ser flexibles en sus expectaciones como padre o madre.

2. Tal vez no sea posible enseñar algunas destrezas a su hijo; su hijo necesita estar listo para la destreza ambos en sus habilidades físicas y mentalmente. Por ejemplo, intentar enseñar a su hijo como leer cuando tiene 2 años, no tiene sentido, cuando le puede enseñar más fácilmente en unos años más cuando este listo.

3. La mayoría de las destrezas son aprendidas paso a paso, cada cual la base para la próxima destreza.

4. Ud. puede apoyar la adquisición de las destrezas de su hijo y su desarrollo por motivándolo y dándole oportunidades de practicar en una manera natural.

ACTIVITY
Effective Coaching During Project Work

Materials

- Pencils and paper
- Handout on Effective Coaching During Project Work
- Strips of paper with one of the coaching/learning situations in number 4 in the list below written on each strip

Directions for Facilitators

Help parents think about coaching project work. Before doing the activity, have parents read "Coaching General Project Skills" on pages 118–121 in *Teaching Your Child to Love Learning*. Or review using the "Effective Coaching During Project Work" handout on the next page.

1. Divide the group into small groups of two, three, or four participants.
2. Have participants divide their paper into three sections by folding it or making lines.
3. At the top of each section, write one of the following headings:

   —Planning and organizing
   —Coaching the use of tools and techniques
   —Using good communication

4. Have each group choose one of the following scenarios to analyze:

   —Mailing a letter
   —Wrapping a birthday present
   —Sorting clothes to be washed
   —Taking a photograph with a camera
   —Making a peanut butter sandwich
   —Making a paper airplane

5. Tell participants to discuss the experience, and write notes under each heading as to what an effective project coach might do.
6. To start the group, the leader should model the example on page 70.
7. Following the activity, have parents share their work. Discuss the benefits of thinking through the learning activity as they take on the role of coach.

Variation for Spanish Speakers

The handout for effective coaching is provided in Spanish on page 74.

Watering Plants in the Garden—
A Mother and Her 3-Year-Old Son

Planning & Organizing: We will need water and a container to get it out to the garden. The container will need to be small enough for my child to control as he waters. The hose might be too hard to handle. I may need to get a child-sized watering can or just use a small can that can be filled from a bucket.

Writing on chart:
Need water & container, container must be small, watering can

Using Tools: I will need to make time to show my child how to water carefully. I might need to explain to my child how to not tip the can too far and get too much water on the plant. I will need to demonstrate.

Writing on chart:
Model not tipping too far and watering small amount slowly

Communication (words modeled to coach the learner): I might say things like "Just give the plant a little drink," "Pour Slowly," or "Now move on to the next plant" if he is watering too much. If he is having trouble with the watering can, I might say "Try using two hands to hold the can." I would want to encourage him by giving specific feedback, "You gave the plant just the amount it needed!"

Writing on the chart:
"Just give a little drink." "Pour slowly" "Try using two hands."

Effective Coaching During Project Work

Coach Your Child in the Use of Tools and Techniques

Model and explain how to use new tools to children.

Without doing it for your child, show and then talk your child through a new technique (for example, hammering a nail).

Be safe!! Modify your plans if a tool or technique is not safe for your child (for example, letting Daddy cut wood instead of showing a child how to use a power saw).

Use Good Communication While Coaching

Remember "doing and learning" is more important than what they make! Tell them that learning to do something like use clay is valuable and more important than making a perfect clay dog.

Repeat your child's words back to him to lessen misunderstandings between the two of you.

Coach your child with positive words that will help her learn new skills and ideas. It is okay to talk your child through her work without doing it for her.

Use specific encouraging language and not just global praise.

Plan and Organize for Coaching

Chose a time when you and your child will be able to work as long as needed. It is frustrating to feel rushed when the work is important!

Think about all the materials needed before you begin.

Be flexible! When delays or disappointments occur—when glue doesn't stick or an expert can't answer questions—be prepared to move on to your next project activity.

Como ser un "entrenador" efectivo durante los proyectos

Uso de las herramientas y las técnicas

Enseñe con ejemplos y explique como usar las herramientas nuevas a sus hijos.

Sin hacerlo para su hijo, enséñale y luego hable con su hijo sobre las técnicas nuevas (para ejemplo: como martillar a los clavos).

¡Tenga cuidado! Puede modificar sus planes si la herramienta es peligrosa para su hijo (por ejemplo: El adulto puede demostrar como cortar la madera en vez de enseñar a su hijo como usar el serrucho mecánico).

Comunicación

Acuérdese, el proceso de "hacer y aprender" es más importante que el artículo que hagan. Por ejemplo, díganles que el proceso de aprender como usar la arcilla vale más que hacer un perro perfecto de arcilla la primera vez.

Repita las palabras de su hijo cuando hablen para evitar confusión entre los dos.

Ayude a su hijo con palabras positivas que le ayudarán con más destrezas e ideas. Está bien hablar con su hijo para ayudarlo con su trabajo pero sin hacerlo para él.

Planificación y organización

Escoja una hora cuando Ud. y su hijo puedan trabajar todo el tiempo necesario. Uno se siente frustrado cuando tiene que hacer un trabajo importante con mucha prisa.

Considere todos los materiales necesarios antes de empezar.

¡Sea flexible! Cuando atrasos o desilusiones ocurran—por ejemplo, cuando la pegadura no pega o un "experto" no puede contestar las preguntas—es importante estar preparado para hacer la próxima actividad en el proyecto.

POWERPOINT® PRESENTATION

FEATURED PROJECT—
THE MEXICAN BAKERY PROJECT

Read the Mexican Bakery Project, pages 77–81 in *Teaching Your Child to Love Learning* to prepare to share this PowerPoint® presentation.

Emphasize the involvement of the all the family in this project and how the parents used the project to also learn English.

This project illustrates

- Topic relevant to the culture of the family
- Second language learning by both children and adults
- Family involvement in making play materials
- Use of scraps and recycled materials

Concepción and her brother Ervin used materials in their art kit to draw pictures about baking. Luz was surprised how much they knew.

The Mexican Bakery Project began when Luz, the mother, noticed how much Concepción liked helping her cook. She thought this would be a good topic for a project. She encouraged Concepción to draw pictures about cooking. Her brother Ervin joined in.

Luz made arrangements for the children to go to the panadería and see how they made Mexican bread.

Luz decided to take the children to a panadería which made traditional Mexican breads and cakes. Luz talked to the owners and they suggested coming when the ovens weren't going so they could go behind the counter.

They saw how they made large numbers of rolls and cakes. They also saw

- How dough was mixed
- Where the dough was put to rise
- How the dough was cut
- Where it went in the ovens
- All the equipment in the bakery

Because Luz scheduled the visit at a time that was convenient for the owners of the bakery, the children were able to see many things demonstrated. The staff took the time to explain things to the children.

They were very interested in the equipment and took photographs to study when they got home.

Photo of the freezer taken by Luz.

Photographs taken on a field-site visit do not have to have the children in them. Pictures like this one can be studied by children when they get home. They can remember what they saw and notice details that they have missed during the visit.

When they came home, Martin, the father, became interested in what they had seen and helped them create models of the equipment.

The mixer in the bakery.   The mixer they made.

Although Martin was unable to go on the field-site visit with his family, the photographs enabled them to share with him what they saw. He helped them create models. He and Luz wrote both the Spanish and the English words on the items as they were also working on learning more English words.

The model that Concepción made of the freezer had moveable shelves with trays of rolls, just like the one at the bakery.

The freezer was a special challenge because it had shelves that moved and rolled. Concepción made her shelves out of a drink box. Modeling clay was used for the miniature rolls and cakes.

Both Concepción and Ervin worked hard on making the models of the equipment.

Children are often motivated to spend hours working on representations for their project because it is something that is interesting to them. This is time well spent because as they work they are thinking about what they learned, using vocabulary words, and building confidence in their skills.

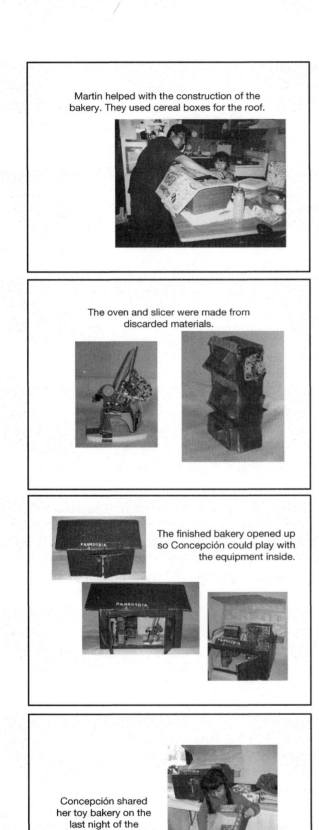

Martin helped with the construction of the bakery. They used cereal boxes for the roof.

The oven and slicer were made from discarded materials.

The finished bakery opened up so Concepción could play with the equipment inside.

Concepción shared her toy bakery on the last night of the project class. She also was able to share it in her preschool classroom where all the children were very impressed.

The family used many scrap and discarded materials in their construction of the models of the bakery equipment.

Although it is obvious that the parents played a large role in designing the equipment, the children did most of the work, and all members of the family worked together on the project. This enabled much discussion about the topic of study and the sharing of many words. The whole family was proud of the outcome.

This elaborate folding model would not have been possible without the help of Martin. His attention and time encouraged the children to work hard. Family projects can involve the whole family and build strong relationships between adults and children.

Sharing of the projects enables children and adults to celebrate the achievement. These experiences build self-confidence in everyone and reinforce the connection between home and school.

POWERPOINT® PRESENTATION

FEATURED PROJECT—THE BUS PROJECT

Read the Bus Project, pages 107–116 in *Teaching Your Child to Love Learning* to prepare to share this PowerPoint® presentation.

This richly described project can be a focus for discussion of developmental appropriateness and for being sensitive to a child's emotional needs.

This project illustrates

- A project with a two-year-old
- Emphasis and understanding of what is developmentally appropriate for a toddler
- Grandparents guiding the project in their home
- A project history book made for the child (this PowerPoint presentation can be printed as individual slides and assembled to make a sample project history book)

The PowerPoint presentation is a copy of a book the grandmother made for her grandson to keep.

Atticus showed an interest in buses when he saw school buses and went with his grandma and grandpa to pick up relatives who came to visit on a bus. Because he has some knowledge about buses and there were several places they could visit buses, the topic appeared to be a good project topic for this two-year-old.

One Saturday when Atticus was staying with his grandparents they took him to Limestone High School where they saw many school buses: big buses, smaller buses, buses from other schools, and one little bus.

You and Grandpa looked at the lights, the mirrors, and the door of the school bus. You even touched the lights on the back of the bus.

We went to Peoria Charter to see the real buses. They were really big!

Here's a bus we made with blocks. You are putting on the lights.

Did your toy bus slide down the yard stick?

Grandma (Mary Ann) and Grandpa (Karl) walked around the parking lot with Atticus, looking at the buses and identifying the parts of the bus that Atticus knew: lights, doors, windows, windshield wipers, and tires. Grandma took many pictures so that she could make a book of bus words for Atticus.

On another day they visited the Charter Bus Company located in a nearby city. When they walked from the parking lot, there was a bus next to the building. Atticus was very interested in touching the parts of the front of bus. However, when they walked around the corner and Atticus saw all of the bus and many buses together, he became overwhelmed and said "Go home, Grandma, go home." Mary Ann realized that these large buses were frightening to him

Atticus was still interested in buses and played bus a lot. Grandma found more toy buses and accessories which would enable Atticus to pretend play. They also read books about buses and sang "The Wheels on the Bus" song.

Atticus incorporated his buses into his play and experimented using them in different ways.

Grandpa is helping you put on the lights. They keep falling off.

You are working on the steering wheel. This one won't stay on.

You painted some on the bus. You didn't want to paint any more.

Put in the key and drive the bus. You drive every day!

After Atticus had been playing buses and reading about buses for some time, Karl brought home a large box. The next time Atticus visited, Mary Ann pulled the box to the center of the room and asked Atticus if he would like to make a bus. Mary Ann brought out books and asked Atticus what he would like to put on the bus. She thought she could be his hands. Atticus got the idea right away and began to direct Mary Ann and Karl to make windows and wheels. (The dialogue during this time is recorded on pages 110 and 111 of *Teaching Your Child to Love Learning.*)

There were many challenges in making the bus. As much as possible, Mary Ann and Karl encouraged Atticus to think of ways to solve them.

Atticus painted some part of the bus but was not interested in painting the whole bus.

Atticus did lots of pretend play in the bus, driving it, putting people in it.

You swept out the inside of your bus. It was dirty.

You had the idea to make a windshield wiper for your bus. You thought of it all by yourself!

We celebrated by showing Daddy and Mommy your bus!

Atticus took care of his bus. Whenever he came to visit, Atticus would ask Karl and Mary Ann to get the bus out for him. They put it away when he was gone.

Mary Ann had some questions about how much Atticus was really imagining it was a bus and whether she and Karl were directing the project rather than Atticus. This changed one day when Atticus took a ladle he was playing with in the kitchen, ran into the living room and held it up with the bowl in the center of the bottom of the windshield and said, "Wiper, Grandma, wiper!" He attached the wiper with masking tape. On another day he used scrap Styrofoam to make a gas tank at the back of his bus and then used his baseball bat to "fill it." These child-initiated events showed that Atticus saw the box as his bus.

Atticus played in his bus for a long time and they continued to explore buses as they came across them in their trips. Atticus's Mom and Dad came to see the bus and listen to Atticus tell them all about it.

UNIT 4

Sharing and Celebrating Projects

POWERPOINT® PRESENTATION

CELEBRATING THE LEARNING

Read Chapter 6 in *Teaching Your Child to Love Learning* before showing this PowerPoint® presentation. This is an introduction to ways that families can culminate project work.

You may want to share this presentation in a workshop series so that parents can prepare to share their project on the last night. As a follow-up to the PowerPoint® presentation, you may want to review pages 18 and 19 of the Family Project Planning Journal.

The PowerPoint® presentation:

- Shows a variety of ways to celebrate
- Revisits projects that have been studied

Family celebrations are the culmination of all the project work and are considered to be a phase three activity.

Gordon's mom, Mimi, carefully documented his project experiences using photos and Gordon's real work. One of the last activities they did together was to organize this scrapbook for Gordon's presentation to his preschool class.

One way children learn more about a project topic is to collect the thing that interests them. During the Ball Project, Reed and Katie collected all different kinds of balls to compare. During the Horse Project, Ashley collected play horses and labeled the different parts.

Murals

As one of their culminating activities, the Schellenburg brothers created a slime mural and represented all the slimy creatures they had discovered during the Slime Project.

Dramatic Play

After lengthy constructions, dramatic play is a perfect way to culminate project work. In this photo, Atticus is really enjoying the play in his school bus construction.

Video Presentations

- Elizabeth's cooking show

Sometimes children want to celebrate their learning in a bigger way. Because the Cooking Project began with watching a cooking show, Elizabeth developed her own cooking show and served her family a recipe she had invented.

Presentations at School

- Joshua shared a poster of his race car project at school.

Many times children are so proud of their project work that they want to share their learning with their friends. As a culminating event, Joshua brought his Race Car project poster to school.

ACTIVITY
Documenting Children's Learning During Project Work

Materials

- Have parents bring a few webs, drawings, paintings, unfinished constructions, photos
- Print slides from one of the PowerPoint® presentations that show products
- Point to pages in the book *Teaching Your Child to Love Learning* that show products
- Sheets of paper (legal-size paper or large sheets of construction paper)
- Handout on next page—"What Evidence Do I Have of My Child's Learning?"

Directions for Facilitators

The purpose of this activity is to help parents understand that the products of their project show what their children are learning and how they can collect that documentation.

1. Share several pieces of documentation either that parents have brought in, out of the book, or printed out from one of the PowerPoint® presentations.
2. Talk about how these things document (or provide evidence) of what children learned.
3. Give each family a piece of paper and have them fold the paper so that there is a fold down the middle parallel to the longest side of the paper.
4. Draw a line down the fold.
5. On the top of the left column write "What happened?"
6. On the top of the right column write "Evidence?"
7. Help the parents think about what happened in the project (for example, read books, took a field trip, interviewed Grandma), and have them write that information in the left column.
8. In the right column, write what evidence they might collect from each activity.

This activity can be done during the project at any time or near the end of the project as part of reflection.

Variations for Family Literacy Programs

The handout on evidence can be shared early in the year and revisited as a reminder of ways that parents can document children's learning. As evidence is collected (photos, drawings, word lists, etc.), these pieces can be used as a focus for writing in journals, or small documentation posters may be made and shared with the class.

The Family Project Planning Journal placed in a three ring binder can also become a scrapbook for documentation if blank paper, photo pages, and page protectors for children's work are added to it.

Variation for Spanish Speakers

The handout on evidence is provided in Spanish on p. 86.

What Evidence Do I Have of My Child's Learning?

1. Photos

On our field-trip?
During our project work?
When we talked to an expert?
When I see my child learning and engaged in his work?
Of big projects, such as constructions made out of cardboard boxes?

2. Paper Items

Drawings?
Writing samples from questions, labels, or observations?
Paintings, posters, or murals?
Word walls or lists of words?
Surveys?

3. My Writing

My child's questions and comments?
Lists my child and I have made?
My web of our project work?
Observations I made while watching my child?

¿Cuales son los indicios que mi niño ha aprendido?

1. Las fotos:

¿Durante las excursiones?

¿Durante nuestro trabajo en el proyecto?

¿Cuándo hablamos con un experto?

¿Cuándo se nota que mi hijo está muy interesado en el trabajo?

¿De los proyectos grandes (por ejemplo: las construcciones de cajas de cartón)?

2. Productos de papel:

¿Los dibujos?

¿La escritura del niño (por ejemplo: las preguntas, las etiquetas, o las observaciones)?

¿Los cuadros, carteles, o murales?

¿Las listas del vocabulario?

¿Las encuestas?

3. La escritura del adulto

¿Las preguntas o comentarios que hizo mi niño?

¿Las listas que mi hijo(a) hicimos juntos?

¿La telaraña de nuestro trabajo en el proyecto?

¿Observaciones que hice mientras observaba a mi hijo(a)?

POWERPOINT® PRESENTATION

FEATURED PROJECT—THE HORSE PROJECT

Read the Horse Project on pages 90–94 in *Teaching Your Child to Love Learning* to prepare to share this PowerPoint® presentation.

This project shows a number of ways of documenting a project, including recording dialogue.

This project illustrates

- A project topic coming from a shared experience
- IEP goals and how a child with special needs can work on these goals during project work
- Illustration of phonetic spelling and letter-like shapes as described on page 125 of *Teaching Your Child to Love Learning*.

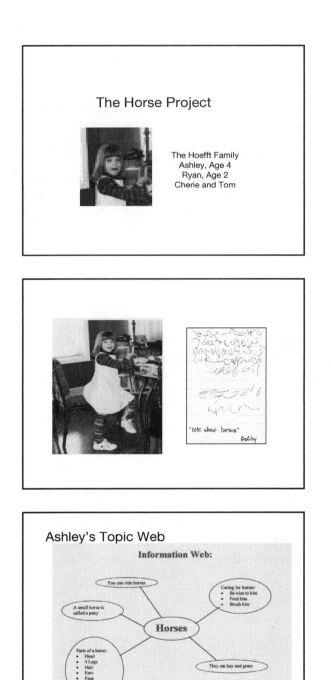

Four-year-old Ashley became interested in horses during a car ride when she noticed a corral of horses.

When Cherie and Ashley made a web about horses, Ashley was interested in the parts of a horse. During later representations, she focused on this aspect of the project.

Ashley's Questions

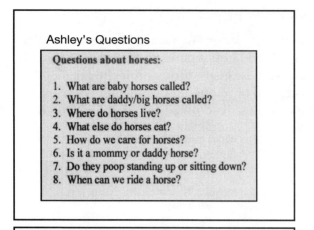

Questions about horses:

1. What are baby horses called?
2. What are daddy/big horses called?
3. Where do horses live?
4. What else do horses eat?
5. How do we care for horses?
6. Is it a mommy or daddy horse?
7. Do they poop standing up or sitting down?
8. When can we ride a horse?

Ashley was interested in the characteristics of a horse. Look how many questions she had!

Labeling the parts of a horse

Ashley spent several project sessions writing labels for her play horses. Because of her cerebral palsy, fine motor activities, especially writing and drawing, were a challenge for her. Development of fine motor skills was part of her IEP (Individualized Educational Plan). The project provided an opportunity to practice at home. Ashley used phonetic spelling to label the parts of horses.

Field-Site Visit

Ashley found the answers to many of her questions on this visit.

During phase two, Ashley and her mother visited a stable where Ashley sketched the horses. Having a clipboard and writing materials encouraged Ashley to draw the horses and stable. It was also her first chance to see a horse up-close.

Field trip to the horse stable, Ashley gets to ride a horse.

During the field trip, the stable owner put Ashley on a horse and they walked around. This was a major thrill for Ashley.

These are both drawings by Ashley. The first drawing was early in the project. The second drawing was after she had seen a real horse and studied the parts of horses.

Time One Drawing

Time Two Drawing

Ashley and her mother made side by side paintings of horses

Ashley's painting

Mother's Painting

Writing horse stories and charts

Celebrating the Project

❑ Invited grandparents to see what they learned about horses
❑ Read a book that Ashley make about what horses eat
❑ Displayed horse drawings
❑ Looked at photos from stable visit
❑ Ended the evening by viewing a video, *Spirit*

Ashley's book of horse food

This is a good example of how a child's drawing reveals what they are learning about a topic. When a parent saves a child's work from the beginning of a project, then asks the child to do the same thing after they have studied the topic, the child's learning becomes visible. Participants can discuss what they think the drawings reveal about what Ashley now knows about horses.

Working side-by-side with children encourages them to try things that they might not try on their own. It is important to model the process of painting but not how to make each line. A parent might say, "I'm going to try to make a tail" rather than demonstrating how to make a tail. It is a good idea to stop often and look at the child's work and say words of encouragement.

During the horse project, Ashley would write stories about the horses she was observing. She wrote these stories by making letter-like shapes. Here she made a chart of people who ride horses. Her mother would also write down what Ashley told her she was writing.

The Hoeffts included the grandparents in a celebration of the horse project. The children displayed their work, and they all watched a video about a horse. This kind of sharing enables grandparents and other adults who are meaningful in a child's life to support those positive dispositions towards learning and achievement. They also see what children find of interest and can then support and talk about that interest with the children.

ACTIVITY
Reflecting on Project Work

Materials

Handout on the next page—Reflecting on Project Work

Directions for Facilitators

1. Pass out the list of questions on the next page, and give the group a moment to look over the questions. If your participants are writers, you might want to let them use the sheet for journaling.
2. Encourage parents to share what they have observed and to talk about their projects. This is a valuable opportunity for everyone to think about what the children have learned, what they as parents have learned, and how they might use the project experience in the future.
3. It is helpful to ask parents to share just a few sentences about each of these questions so no one can dominate the discussion.
4. Be sure as a facilitator to make positive comments about each project and draw out the positive experiences for children.

Variation

It might also be helpful to put the questions on an overhead or on chart paper on the wall to keep the conversation focused.

Fewer than 10 Participants

If you have 10 or fewer participants, this reflection can occur in a whole group with the facilitator monitoring. Sharing with the whole group might also be helpful for parents who need or want more guidance.

Groups Larger than 10

For groups larger than 10, the group may be divded into smaller groups to share relections. If you have more than one facilitator, each facilitator can take a group.

Variation for Spanish Speakers

The handout on reflecting on project work is also provided in Spanish on p. 92.

Reflecting on Project Work

What do you think was the most meaningful part of the project for your child?

Is there anything you might have done differently?

What did you learn about your child during this project?

What did you learn about parenting during this project?

Una última consideración para los padres de familia

¿Cuál parte del proyecto fue la más importante para su hijo(a)?

¿Cuándo hagan proyectos en el futuro, que hará Ud. diferente?

¿Qué aprendió Ud. sobre las fortalezas y intereses de su niño durante el proyecto?

¿Qué aprendió Ud. sobre ser un padre de familia durante el proyecto?

ACTIVITY
Sharing of Project Documentation

Materials

Have space available for each family to share their projects. You may wish to assign spaces or let parents choose where to put their work. Have poster board available to tack things to, if needed. Have table space available.

Directions for Facilitators

Sharing and seeing other project work is an important part of learning how to do projects. You may wish to have parents share alone, bring children to help them share, or you may wish to provide child care and have parents share alone and then have children join them for a celebration. This should be a celebratory event.

Have a handout or put the following items on the board or overhead:

1. What are three of the most important things that happened in your project?

    —Did you interview an expert? Visit somewhere?
    —Did you make anything?
    —What did the children learn?
    —(If children are present, involve them in sharing their work.)

2. Assign a time keeper to be sure everyone gets equal time to share. Be sure as a facilitator to make positive comments about each project and to draw out the positive experiences for children. If parents are uncomfortable "giving reports," have the projects displayed, then gather around the projects and let participants ask questions.

Fewer than 10 Participants

If you have 10 or fewer participants, this sharing can occur in a whole group with the facilitator monitoring. Sharing with the whole group might also be helpful for parents who need or want more guidance.

Groups Larger than 10

For larger groups you can set up project displays (have poster paper handy). Everyone can walk around and see all the projects. Then the group can be subdivided into small groups of no more than five or six to share their projects. If you have more than one facilitator, each facilitator can take a group.

About the Authors

Judy Harris Helm, Ed.D. assists schools and early childhood programs in integrating research and new methods through her consulting and training company, Best Practices, Inc. She began her career teaching first grade, then taught, directed, and designed early childhood and primary programs, as well as trained teachers at the community college, undergraduate, and graduate level. She served on the Task Force for the design of the Valeska Hinton Early Childhood Education Center, a state of the art urban collaboration school for children age three through first grade in Peoria, Illinois, and then became Professional Development Coordinator for the school. She is past state President of the Illinois Association for the Education of Young Children. Dr. Helm is co-author of *Windows on Learning: Documenting Children's Work*; *Teacher Materials for Documenting Children's Work*; *Young Investigators: The Project Approach in the Early Years*; and co-editor of *The Power of Projects*. She is the mother of Amanda and Rebecca, now grown, who thrived on project work.

Stacy Berg, M.A. has been the director of Northminster Learning Center since 1999. Her academic background includes a bachelor's degree in Early Childhood Education and a master's degree in Curriculum and Instruction, both from Bradley University. Stacy began the programs at Northminster after previously teaching in at-risk preschool programs. Along with presenting at education conferences nationally, she enjoys consulting and collaborating with fellow educators and programs. Stacy and her husband Andy have three children—Drew, a first-grader, Seth, a preschooler, and Jena, a toddler.

Pam Scranton, M.A., the curriculum and training coordinator for Northminster Learning Center, is in her 19th year as an early childhood educator. Pam is responsible for supporting early childhood teaching staff, designing developmentally appropriate curriculum, and implementing documentation, authentic assessment, and project trainings. She is a frequent presenter in school districts on topics such as engaging children in project work, authentic assessment, documentation, and developmentally appropriate practice. She is a contributing author of The Power of Projects. Pam is the mother of teenager Lauren, and two elementary-age boys, Joey and Alex.

Rebecca Wilson, B.A. is recipient of the Irving B. Harris Fellowship at Erikson Institute where she is in a masters program in Early Childhood and Bilingual/ ESL Education. She taught prekindergarten, and kindergarten, and served as coordinator in the Spanish Dual Language program in West Liberty, Iowa. In addition, Ms. Wilson taught in a state at-risk prekindergarten program, with children speaking several different languages, in Illinois. She is certified in Early Childhood Education, Bilingual Ed./ESL, and also secondary Spanish. Ms. Wilson presents at conferences and provides consultation on bilingual education and ESL, as well as on the project approach. She is author of the chapter "Meeting the Needs of Second Language Learners" in *The Power of Projects* and has published articles nationally and internationally.

The following pages contain the Family Project Planning Journal from *Teaching Your Child to Love Learning* in a larger format than in the book. The journal can be photocopied and put in a three-ring binder for each workshop participant. Add blank paper for notes and observations, sheet protectors, and pens and pencils. Following the English version, the Family Project Planning Journal is also provided in Spanish.

THE FAMILY PROJECT PLANNING JOURNAL

This journal accompanies

Teaching Your Child to Love Learning: A Guide to Doing Projects at Home

JUDY HARRIS HELM
STACY BERG
PAM SCRANTON

HOW TO RAISE CHILDREN
WHO LOVE TO LEARN

This journal is designed to be used with the chapters in this book, *Teaching Your Child to Love Learning: A Guide to Doing Projects at Home*. The purpose of the journal is to help you support your child's project work and record results. This journal should be copied and inserted in a loose-leaf binder with pocket pages or scrapbook pages for collecting children's work.

THE PROJECT APPROACH

What is the project approach?

The project approach is an in-depth study of a particular topic by a child or group of children. The project approach structure was developed by Dr. Lilian Katz at the University of Illinois.

How is it different from other ways of learning?

In project work your child will study a topic of interest for a long time period. You will select a topic that your child is interested in and is meaningful to him in his life. Your child will go into great depth in his study and often at a level higher than many adults would expect for his age.

How will your child learn?

Your child will use a variety of ways to find answers to questions. These include traditional resources like books. Other resources usually include field-site visits and/or interviews with experts. An expert is anyone who knows a great deal about the topic. Your child will plan questions for interviews and have tasks to do on field-site visits. Your child may also make field notes and draw or write on-site. She may also make plans for building things and engage in pretend play about the topic, which helps her sort out what she is learning.

Your child will do problem solving with you structuring problems and assisting in finding solutions and resources. Your child will redraw and rewrite as more is learned. Some of the ways that children record their learning are project books, murals, artwork, constructions, and journals.

THE PROJECT APPROACH FOR FAMILIES

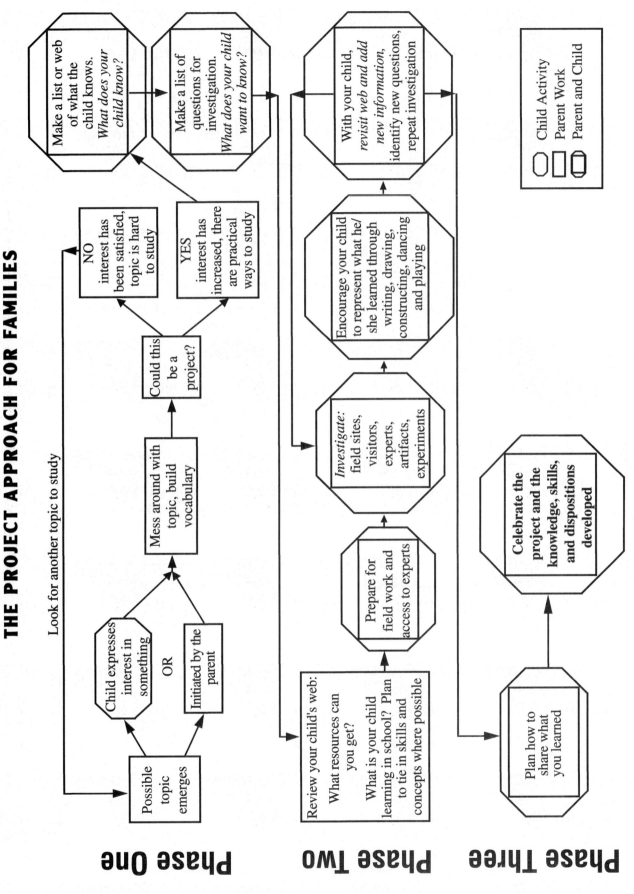

Phase One

Possible topic emerges

Child expresses interest in something
OR
Initiated by the parent

Mess around with topic, build vocabulary

Could this be a project?

NO interest has been satisfied, topic is hard to study

YES interest has increased, there are practical ways to study

Look for another topic to study

Make a list or web of what the child knows. *What does your child know?*

Make a list of questions for investigation. *What does your child want to know?*

Phase Two

Review your child's web: What resources can you get? What is your child learning in school? Plan to tie in skills and concepts where possible

Prepare for field work and access to experts

Investigate: field sites, visitors, experts, artifacts, experiments

Encourage your child to represent what he/she learned through writing, drawing, constructing, dancing and playing

With your child, *revisit web and add new information,* identify new questions, repeat investigation

Phase Three

Plan how to share what you learned

Celebrate the project and the knowledge, skills, and dispositions developed

Child Activity
Parent Work
Parent and Child

Phase One

GETTING STARTED WITH YOUR PROJECT

IDENTIFYING YOUR CHILD'S INTEREST

The project topic is determined by your child's interest. Projects can start in two ways:

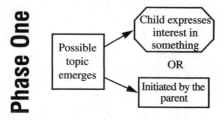

Young children (2–4 years) show you they are interested in a subject by

- Asking questions
- Requesting information
- Pushing forward to look at something
- Picking up items
- Hoarding "souvenirs"
- Focusing on things for a longer time than usual
- Attending carefully to what others say about a subject

School-age children (5 years and up) show they are interested by

- Asking questions (How does that work? What is that for? What does he do?)
- Asking for information
- Spending time examining items
- Saving items
- Starting collections
- Paying more attention to conversations about the topic
- Requesting to go places that relate to the topic (such as an airport)

Parent Journal: What are some interests that I have observed in my child in the past?

WHEN YOUR CHILD APPEARS TO HAVE AN INTEREST

If your child seems to be interested in something, like trucks, you can try out that topic as a project. Encourage your child to think more about it. Mess around with the topic. This provides background knowledge for both of you. For example, with the topic of trucks you could

With Younger Children

- Talk about trucks
- Read a book about trucks
- Play trucks together
- Help your child draw pictures of trucks
- Look at real trucks in parking lots, etc.
- Collect brochures, diagrams, photos
- Provide parts and pieces of real trucks

With Older Children

- Involve children in doing adult tasks related to trucks
- Provide parts and pieces of real trucks
- Provide access to real tools related to trucks
- Take children on a mini-field-site visit (for example, to watch someone change oil)
- Provide nonfiction books about trucks
- Collect brochures, diagrams, and any print sources about trucks

If your child's curiosity is satisfied or if the child doesn't show much interest, look for another topic. If your child shows signs of still being interested, you may have a project!

WHEN YOUR CHILD DOESN'T APPEAR TO HAVE A PARTICULAR INTEREST

Children, even in primary school, don't always show interests on their own. Often a child may need to be encouraged to focus on something and to think about it so that an interest may develop. If you don't see any signs of interest in a specific topic, you can try interesting your child in something by doing one of the following:

- ❏ Read a book
- ❏ Talk about a topic
- ❏ Share your own interest in a topic
- ❏ Watch a video
- ❏ Show him concrete objects
- ❏ Vist a place where you can observe or see objects or things

Be sure to choose a topic that your child wants to know about! Without your child's interest, it will not become a project. Be sure to take time to find something that your child wants to know about.

Parent Journal: What is my child interested in? What does he want to know about?

HOW TO DECIDE IF AN INTEREST IS A GOOD PROJECT TOPIC

1. A good project topic includes real objects. Children enjoy touching, moving, and using real objects in their play. Children learn by touching, moving, carrying, modeling, hearing, tasting, and looking closely. Choose a project topic that has many real things that are safe to handle, not just ideas. For example, fire trucks is a better project than fire fighting; mirrors is a better topic than reflections.

2. A good project topic is connected to something your child knows about. Children like to learn about things they already know something about. It is hard for young children to think about topics for which they have little experience or words. Boats might be a good topic if your child has been in a real boat but not so good if he has never seen a boat. Think about your child's daily life. What does he see? Where does she go? What is around your neighborhood? For example, the ocean is not a good topic if you live in the middle of the United States.

3. A good project topic can be investigated at a place you can visit, preferably again and again. Children, especially young children, benefit from seeing real places. If a child can only learn about something from books or photos he can develop unrealistic ideas. For example, studying the ocean without ever visiting it might result in a number of misunderstandings. Think broadly about places to visit. A field-site visit might be a short walk to your garage or to the shop at the end of your street. Your child will also benefit by going to places again and again. When you first take your child to the zoo, he may have difficulty focusing on just the monkeys, but after a visit or two the rest of the zoo won't be so distracting. When you choose a topic for project work, think about where you might visit. Learning how your lawnmower works might be a better topic than studying airplanes, which requires a trip to the airport, because you can easily go to see a real lawnmower and you can do it over and over again.

4. A good project topic can be researched by your child. Research for young children consists of observing, manipulating, experimenting, asking questions, trying out ideas, and visiting places. Young children are less interested when they have to listen or learn only through books, videos, encyclopedias, or what an adult tells them. Your child will learn more when she can "study" a topic herself (touch, poke, turn, etc.). It works best if you can be a resource and help your child rather than be a lecturer on the topic.

5. A good project topic enables your child to use skills and methods appropriate for his age. Children like to share what they know through drawings, paintings, sculptures, or playing. Young children especially like to make play places, such as a McDonald's restaurant, where they can pretend. Is there something that your child could draw, paint, make a model of, or use for pretend play?

6. A good project topic is worth studying. Projects take time and effort; so, what children study should be worth learning about. For example, learning the characters in a favorite video may be interesting, but it won't help develop school skills or interest in school subjects. It would be better to learn how a car works or what happens in a grocery store than to do a project on a movie character. This is especially true if interest in school is an issue with your child.

7. A good project topic is related to your child's world. Projects should help children learn about their daily world and their family and community. The world of young children is very small—family, neighborhood, and school or care center. Projects that are based on family interests are especially meaningful. If there is a family tradition of fishing, and many adults in your family fish, this could be a great project.

Teaching Your Child to Love Learning, Copyright © 2004 by Teachers College, Columbia University

Parent Journal: Mess around with the topic. What happened? Is my child still interested?

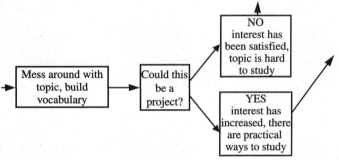

Mess around with topic, build vocabulary → Could this be a project?

NO
interest has been satisfied, topic is hard to study

YES
interest has increased, there are practical ways to study

Parent Journal: Is this a good topic for us to consider as a project? Why or why not?

FIND OUT WHAT YOUR CHILD
UNDERSTANDS ABOUT THE TOPIC

The more you talk about the topic with your child, the more you will know what your child might have questions about. This will give you ideas of whom to talk to and where you might like to visit.

What does my child know about this topic?

You can keep a record of what he knows and what he learns by

- Making a web
- Making a list of questions
- Saving drawings
- Photographing things he builds
- Writing down what he says

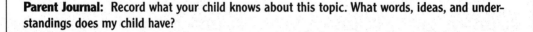

Make a list or web of what the child knows. *What does your child know?*

Make a list of questions for investigation. *What does your child want to know?*

Parent Journal: Record what your child knows about this topic. What words, ideas, and understandings does my child have?

FORM QUESTIONS FOR INVESTIGATING

It is important for your child to find answers to her own questions. Your child may surprise you with what she wants to know. For example, she may want to know where the firefighter eats his dinner or what the fisherman does with his fish. Because you want your child to **think**, it is important that she research what **she** wants to find out. This is how you can support the development of your child's curiosity and intellectual dispositions.

You can help your child learn to form a question by doing the following:

Looking at a book on the topic, you could say (fill in the blanks appropriately for your topic):

- What things in that picture do you want to know about?
  What is _____ ?
- Where do you think _____ ? Would you like to know that?
- Who do you think that is? Would you like to know who does _____ ?
- When do you think the _____ does _____ ?
- Why do they _____ ? Why does he _____ ?

You can also model questions:

- I would like to know what that is. I would like to know what that is used for.
- I wonder how the mechanic gets rusted bolts off of the car.

Parent Journal: What questions does my child have about this topic?

SETTING THE STAGE

As you prepare for the investigation phase, you will have a number of considerations about the work environment, materials, and time. Each of these issues can be addressed with thoughtful planning and organization.

1. How can I provide an environment for meaningful learning?
   ❏ Where is there enough space for my child and me to work together?
   ❏ Where will I be comfortable working alongside my child?
   ❏ Where will my child have a surface to write, draw, paint, and use materials like clay?

2. As you prepare to gather materials you will need for project work, the following questions will help you collect basic supplies and tools you will need.
   ❏ What will we write and draw with? (ex. markers, chalk, crayons, pens, pencils)
   ❏ What will we write and draw on? (ex. paper, chalkboard, old envelopes, note cards)
   ❏ What will we paint with? (ex. sponges, brushes)
   ❏ What will we use to hold things together? (ex. glue, tape, tacky glue, staples, brads)
   ❏ What will we cut with? (ex. child scissors, adult scissors)
   ❏ What will we use to sculpt? (ex. clay, wire, play dough)
   ❏ What will use to clean up our mess? (ex. paper towels, sponges, baby wipes)

3. How can I store materials for projects and other forms of meaningful learning?
   ❏ Where will we keep paper, clay, and books about project topics?
   ❏ Where can ongoing work be stored so that it is safe from siblings, vacuum cleaners, or the dog?
   ❏ Where can materials be stored neatly and safely but so that they are still accessible to my child?

4. How will I prepare a literacy-rich environment for project work?
   ❏ Where is a flat surface for writing and drawing with enough room to lay out reference books?
   ❏ Do I have writing tools like pens, pencils, fine-line markers, and colored pencils readily available to encourage writing?
   ❏ Do I have different kinds and sizes of writing paper for writing, making signs, and labeling readily available to encourage writing?
   ❏ Do I have a picture dictionary?
   ❏ Do I have a tub, basket, or shelf that can be used just for books on project topics?
   ❏ Where can I go to get reference books? Do I know where my library is located, and do I have a card?
   ❏ Where can I get on the Internet to get information for my child?

5. How can I provide the time for projects and other forms of meaningful learning?
   ❏ When can we reserve time so we can really concentrate on our project work?
   ❏ Are there short blocks of time when we could fit in project work, such as a stop at the library or a drawing session?

6. How will I document my child's learning?
   ❏ Do I have a camera or video camera to record field sites and my child's work?
   ❏ Do I have a place to display my child's work?
   ❏ How will I keep a history of the project?

MATERIALS AND SUPPLIES

As you begin your collection of materials, check out the following list to see what you might currently have at home and what items you might want to purchase or borrow. Keep in mind that you will never need all of these items for every project. Different projects will lend themselves to the use of different materials.

Aluminum foil	Fabric	Q-tips
Art smock	Feathers	Ribbon
Balloons	Felt	Rubber bands
Balls	Film canisters	Ruler
Beads	Foam	Scissors
Beans	Glitter	Sponges
Bottle caps	Glue	Stapler
Boxes	Hole punch	Stencils
Brads	Lace	String
Buttons	Lids	Tape—clear, packing
Cardboard	Masking tape	Thread
Ceramic tiles	Nails	Tissue paper
Chalk	Newspaper	Toothpicks
Clay	Noodles, dry	Wallpaper scraps
Clothespins	Markers—thin, fat	Wrapping paper
Coffee filters	Modeling clay (e.g., Sculpey)	Yarn
Construction paper	Paint—tempera, watercolors	
Cotton balls	Pencils	Additional ideas:
Crepe paper	Pipe cleaners	
Egg cartons	Popsicle sticks	

As you explore your topic, children will often need a medium to sculpt or mold. While many commercial materials such as Model Magic by Crayola or Sculpey modeling compound can be purchased, you may want to consider using the simple, homemade play dough recipe below.

Homemade Play Dough Recipe*

2 cups of flour
1 cup of salt
A few drops of food coloring
2 tablespoons of alum (do not substitute)
2 cups of boiling water

1. Mix the dry ingredients in a mixing bowl. Put water on to boil and add the food coloring to the water.
2. Add the boiling water to the dry ingredients. Allow the water to soak in for a couple of minutes while it cools.
3. After a few minutes, begin to knead the mixture. The more you knead the dough, the smoother the consistency will be. Store in an airtight container.

*Be very exact in the measurements

Phase Two

INVESTIGATING YOUR TOPIC

WHAT DO YOU HOPE YOUR CHILD WILL LEARN?

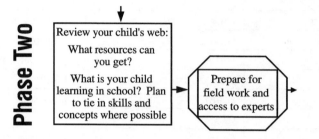

There is one last thing for you to do before you begin the most exciting phase of the project work, investigation. Take some time to think about what you want your child to learn from this experience.

Parent Journal: What do I hope my child will learn from these investigations?

PREPARE FOR FIELD WORK

Now is the time to think about places that you can visit with your child to investigate this topic. Where could you go to learn?

How will I help my child focus his investigation?

❏ Discussion
❏ List of questions
❏ List of tasks to do

This is when you will help your child learn new information about the topic and get her questions answered. You may visit a place; have conversations with someone who has expertise; and collect real objects, books, or photographs. A field-site visit provides a shared event. You can coach your child in using the skills of observing, talking, drawing, painting, and sketching. Encourage your child to ask the questions the two of you prepared.

You may want to think how you can prepare your child for this experience:

❏ Discuss it with her in advance
❏ Practice skills such as drawing or photographing
❏ Remind your child about the purpose of the visit and about the questions
❏ Rehearse asking questions

Parent Journal: What specific experiences do I want my child to have on a field-site visit? What specific discoveries do I want to occur?

IDENTIFYING AND FINDING EXPERTS

In good project work, children interact with adults (or even older children) to find answers to their questions and to learn from them. An "expert" in project work refers to anyone who has more knowledge about the topic than the child. It is more important to find experts who can talk to the child on her level than to find experts with "recognized expertise." For example, Uncle Harry, who has a new pick up truck and is interested in talking about trucks with your child, would be a better expert than a community college automotive instructor.

What expertise do we need for this project? What does someone need to know about this topic to be an expert for my child?

❑ What skills will the expert be able to share?
❑ Does he have real objects that he could lend to my child for investigation?
❑ Does she have time to spend with my family?
❑ Is he up to the activity level involved? (For example, Grandpa may be able to give great advice regarding fishing lures but not be able to hike along a trout stream.)
❑ Is this person someone I want my child to spend time with? (Experts are often seen as role models. It is wise to think about this when establishing contact.)

Parent Journal: What kind of "expert" do we need? Where might I find one?

TAKING YOUR CHILD ON A FIELD EXPERIENCE

Do I need to arrange for transportation to a site? Do I need to let the appropriate person at the site know we are coming? How can I let him know what my child is studying and what we want to know?

1 to 2 weeks before the visit:
Do I need to
❑ Phone the site   or   ❑ Scout it out
❑ Prepare a sibling to go along   or   ❑ Arrange for care of siblings

Think about discussing with your field-site expert:
- Safety issues involved in this site visit or expert visit
- Importance of your child investigating and being able to ask questions
- Overview of what your child currently knows and understands and what she is interested in learning
- Importance of concrete real objects, especially those that your child can interact with
- How your child will be recording what she learns—Tape recording? Video? Clipboards? Writing? Photographing?
- Items or scenes that your child may want to spend some time sketching, recording, etc. (Be sure to allow enough time in your visit for sketching, manipulating real objects, etc. Plan the visit so your child does not feel hurried.)
- Any tools, equipment, products, etc. that can be borrowed for further investigation

Notes:

On the day of the visit:
Materials and supplies needed:
_____ Clipboards
_____ Recording equipment: ❑ camera   ❑ video   ❑ tape recorder
_____ Paper, pencils, art materials
_____ Bags, boxes, or other containers for materials collected
_____ Other

As your child investigates and visits field sites, she may develop new questions. You may need to provide additional resources to meet this need.

Parent Journal: What additional questions does my child have?

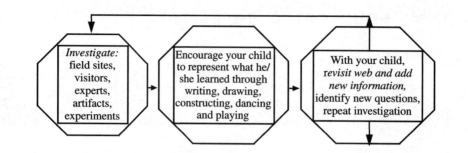

HELPING YOUR CHILD REPRESENT
WHAT HE IS LEARNING

How will my child review his experiences and field work?

❏ Discuss sketches   ❏ Time 1/Time 2 drawings   ❏ Review photos   ❏ Dictate experience

❏ Revise webs   ❏ List answers to questions   ❏ Scrapbook   ❏ Display

How will I focus my child on other resources?

❏ Introduce new books   ❏ Add more concrete things related to the topic   ❏ Encourage play

How can my child represent what he has learned about the topic?

❏ Drawings/sketches   ❏ Paintings   ❏ Constructions   ❏ Play   ❏ Language products

What do I need to do to encourage representation?

How can I foster the following experiences through this project?

❏ Problem Solving: What can my child figure out on his own?

❏ Development of construction skills such as taping, gluing, and organizing materials?

Parent Journal: If your child is school age, what school skills might be used in this project?

Reading:

Writing and spelling:

Math:

Science or social studies:

What additional resources can you bring into your home so that your child can find more information and learn at a deeper level of study?

❑ Books
❑ Construction Materials
❑ Adults to interview
❑ Objects to play with and take apart

Is there one aspect or part of the topic that your child seems especially interested in, such as a part of a car or the checkout scanner? Can you study this aspect or object in more depth?

Phase Three

CELEBRATING THE LEARNING

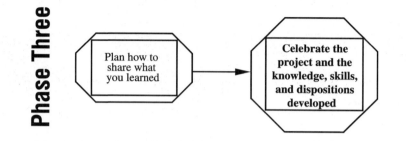

Phase Three

Plan how to share what you learned → Celebrate the project and the knowledge, skills, and dispositions developed

All projects come to an end. This is a natural process. Some projects will be short, while other projects may extend for months. It is time to end a project when you can answer "yes" to any of these questions:

_____ Is my child satisfied with what she has learned about the topic?

_____ Would further investigation require more skills than my child can learn at this age—such as car repair or driving?

_____ Has my child lost interest in the topic?

WHY WE CULMINATE AND CELEBRATE

Although all projects eventually end, they should be celebrated in some way. Looking back at what has been learned and accomplished in a project builds your child's self-confidence. It helps your child identify what it means to learn and the feelings of satisfaction that come from learning. Celebrating provides a sense of closure. The process of celebrating can create memories that will be treasured for years to come.

Don't be surprised if your child's interest wanes and she doesn't finish a project. Remember the important thing is that the child **thinks, investigates, and sees herself as a learner.** It is not necessary for children to finish every project. Young children will explore lots of interests before they find what they especially like. When they do a project, interest in the topic can last for years and even become a vocation.

EVIDENCE OF LEARNING

It is helpful to take time to make a collection of what your child has learned and what skills she has developed. This can be documented by

❏ Drawings/sketches ❏ Webs ❏ Paintings
❏ Lists ❏ Constructions ❏ Murals
❏ Play ❏ Photographs ❏ Making a collection
❏ Language products (such as writing diagrams, charts, posters)

CELEBRATE THE PROJECT

Projects usually end with some way to capture and remember the experience. Your child may

- Make models
- Start a scrapbook
- Play out the experience (while you take photos)
- Start a collection
- Paint pictures
- Take photos
- Draw pictures
- Make a video
- Share what he has learned with neighbors and friends
- Present what he has learned to his class at school

Young children won't know how to do these things the first time, and you will have to help your child make a scrapbook or show him how he can collect items. Remember, however, to let your child take the lead. The scrapbook may not be neat or the model may not look much like the real thing. It is important, however, that your child do the work and feel good about the experience.

Parent Journal: Culminating the project. What ways might I help my child culminate this project so that we all have a sense of accomplishment?

THE NEXT PROJECT

Parent Journal: Is there another topic that has emerged for further investigation? Could we investigate this topic now or at a later time?

LAST THOUGHT FOR PARENTS

Parent Journal: What did I learn from sharing this experience with my child? What did I learn about my child's strengths and interests? How might I support my child's meaningful learning in the future?

EL DIARIO DE LOS PROYECTOS PARA LA FAMILIA

Una guía para los padres de familia
Este diario acompaña el libro

*Teaching Your Child to Love Learning:
A Guide to Doing Projects at Home*

JUDY HARRIS HELM
STACY BERG
PAM SCRANTON
Traducido por: **REBECCA WILSON**

EL LIBRO

¿Qué es este libro?

Este libro es un diario de los proyectos que ocurren en una familia. Acompaña el libro *Teaching Your Child to Love Learning: A Guide to Doing Projects at Home*. El propósito del libro es ayudar a los padres de familia mientras hacen un proyecto. El libro provee una introducción a como hacer los proyectos paso por paso. También ayuda a los padres de familia a planear y notar los resultados del proyecto.

EL MÉTODO DE PROYECTO

¿Qué es el método llamado proyecto?

Un proyecto es una investigación en profundidad por un grupo de niños o por un solo niño. Aprender con los proyectos no es nuevo. Lilian Katz de la Universidad de Illinois desarrolló la estructura del método llamado proyecto.

¿Cómo es diferente de otras maneras de aprender?

Los niños estudian un tema por un tiempo largo. El tema es elegido por los niños porque se interesa y tiene importancia en sus vidas. Los estudiantes estudian el tema profundamente y muchas veces a un nivel más alto de que piensan los adultos alguien de esta edad joven puede lograr.

¿Cómo planean?

Los estudiantes hacen sus propios planes con la ayuda de un adulto. Los planes normalmente incluyen una excursión o una entrevista con un experto. Un experto es una persona quien sabe mucho sobre el tema.

¿Cómo aprenden?

Los niños usan muchos recursos para buscar respuestas a sus preguntas, que incluyen recursos tradicionales como libros. También hacen investigaciones en una excursión. Los niños hacen preguntas para las entrevistas y tienen tareas para cada excursión o cada entrevista. Hacen notas y dibujos durante la excursión o visita del experto al salón de clase. Luego, hacen planes para una construcción o una obra que les ayudan a pensar en lo que han aprendido.

A menudo durante el proyecto, los niños resuelven problemas ellos solos. El adulto les ayuda a investigar y buscar más recursos de información. Los dibujarán y escribirán de nuevo mientras crece su conocimiento. Unas maneras de notar su conocimiento son libros del proyecto, murales, obras de arte, construcciones, y diarios.

EL MÉTODO LLAMADO PROYECTO PARA LAS FAMILIAS

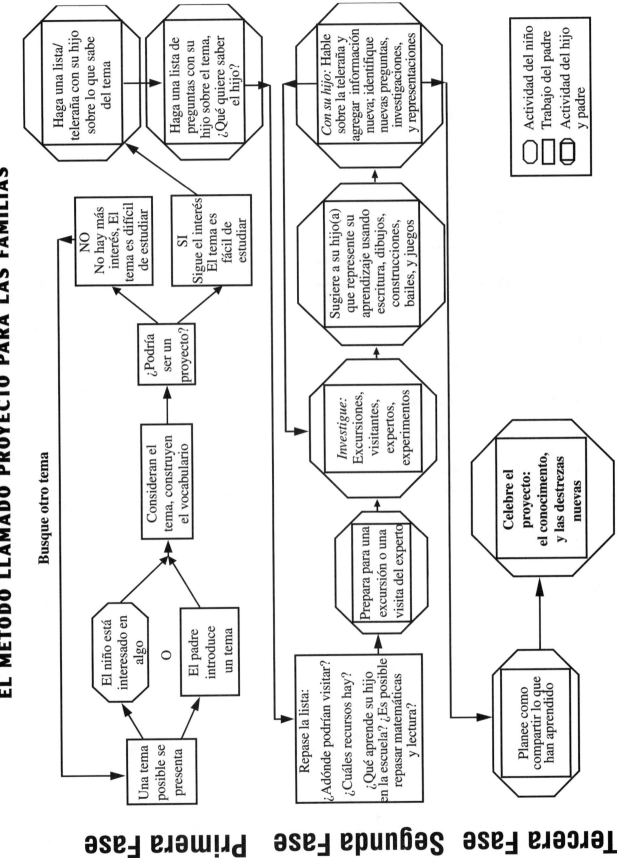

Primera Fase

Una tema posible se presenta

El niño está interesado en algo

O

El padre introduce un tema

Consideran el tema, construyen el vocabulario

¿Podría ser un proyecto?

NO
No hay más interés, El tema es difícil de estudiar

SI
Sigue el interés
El tema es fácil de estudiar

Busque otro tema

Haga una lista/telaraña con su hijo sobre lo que sabe del tema

Haga una lista de preguntas con su hijo sobre el tema, ¿Qué quiere saber el hijo?

Segunda Fase

Repase la lista:
¿Adónde podrían visitar?
¿Cuáles recursos hay?
¿Qué aprende su hijo en la escuela? ¿Es posible repasar matemáticas y lectura?

Prepara para una excursión o una visita del experto

Investigue:
Excursiones, visitantes, expertos, experimentos

Sugiere a su hijo(a) que represente su aprendizaje usando escritura, dibujos, construcciones, bailes, y juegos

Con su hijo: Hable sobre la telaraña y agregar información nueva; identifique nuevas preguntas, investigaciones, y representaciones

Tercera Fase

Planee como compartir lo que han aprendido

Celebre el proyecto:
el conocimiento, y las destrezas nuevas

Actividad del niño
Trabajo del padre
Actividad del hijo y padre

Teaching Your Child to Love Learning, Copyright © 2004 by Teachers College, Columbia University

La primera fase:

COMO EMPEZAR EL PROYECTO

El tema de los proyectos viene del interés de su hijo.

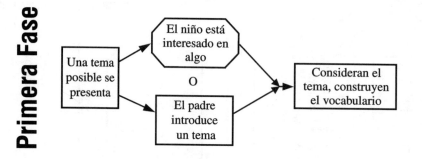

Los niños de 2–4 años nos enseña su interés por:

- Preguntar para información (¿Qué es?)
- Acercarse para ver algo mejor
- Agarrar a un objeto
- Prestar mucha atención por un largo tiempo
- Escuchar con mucha atención cuando alguien hable sobre un tema

Los niños de 5–8 años nos enseña su interés por:

- Preguntas (¿Cómo funciona? ¿Para qué es? ¿Qué hace el señor o la señora?)
- Escoger libros sobre un tema
- Preguntar para más información
- Examinar objetos
- Prestar mucha atención a una conversación sobre un tema
- Sugerir excursiones para aprender más.

¿QUÉ HAGO CUANDO MI HIJO(A) ESTÁ INTERESADO(A)?

Si su hijo(a) tiene un interés, por ejemplo de los camiones, pueden probar el tema. Ayude a su hijo(a) *pensar más* en el tema. *Experimente con el tema*.

Abajo se encuentra unos ejemplos de lo que podrían hacer para empezar un proyecto sobre los camiones.

Con niños más pequeños

- hable sobre los camiones
- lea un libro sobre los camiones
- juegue a los camiones juntos
- dibuje unos camiones
- busque fotos de camiones

Con los niños más grandes

- permita a su hijo en ayudar con el camión/carro
- introduzca partes verdaderos de un camión
- enseñe a su hijo(a) las herramientas de un camión
- mire a unos camiones
- lea unos libros sobre los camiones

Si su hijo(a) no tiene mucha curiosidad o no aparece ser interesadota sobre el tema, busque otro tema.

¡Si su hijo(a) aparece ser muy interesado(a) o tiene muchas preguntas, podría ser un buen tema para un proyecto!

¿QUÉ HAGO SI MI HIJO NO ESTÁ INTERESADO EN NINGÚN TEMA?

A veces los niños necesitan ayuda en buscar un interés. Para ayudarles podría:

- ❏ Leer un libro
- ❏ Hablar sobre el tema
- ❏ Compartir su propio interés en un tema
- ❏ Visitar un lugar donde pueden observar
- ❏ Mirar un video
- ❏ Enseñarle algo especial

Es muy importante descubrir el interés de su hijo! Si él no está interesado, no va a querer hacer ningún proyecto.

Diario del padre de familia: ¿En qué está interesado mi hijo? ¿De qué quiere saber?

¿CÓMO DECIDO SI ES UN BUEN TEMA PARA UN PROYECTO?

Hay unos temas que no son buenos para los proyectos. Abajo se encuentra unas sugerencias sobre como escoger los temas.

1. Un buen tema para un proyecto tiene muchos objetos tangibles. A los niños les gusta tocar, mover, y jugar con los objetos de un tema.

2. Un buen tema tiene que ver con algo que es parte de la vida del niño. Es difícil empezar un tema si el niño no tiene un poco de experiencia y palabras.

3. Los proyectos son mejores si tienen que ver con una parte de la vida diaria.

4. Los mejores proyectos resultan cuando los niños pueden investigar independiente de los adultos (o sea los temas en que se pueda tocar, ver, etc.).

5. Los niños aprenden mejor cuando pueden estudiar de una manera apropiada para sus edades.

6. Es mejor si el tema vale la pena estudiar.

7. El tema del proyecto debe ser parte de su vida.

Diario para el padre de familia: ¿Es este tema apropiado para un proyecto?

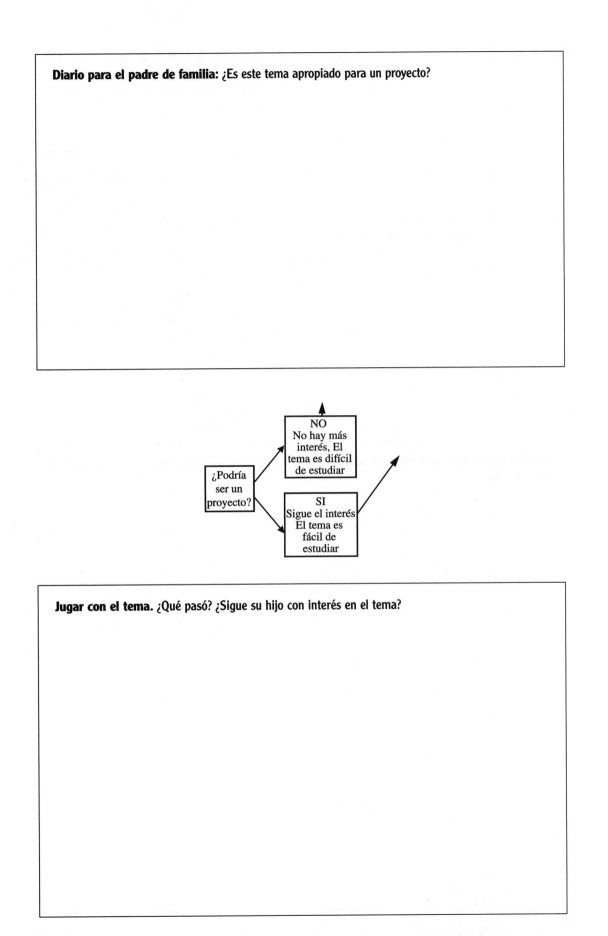

```
                              NO
                          No hay más
                           interés, El
         ¿Podría          tema es difícil
         ser un           de estudiar
        proyecto?
                              SI
                          Sigue el interés
                          El tema es
                          fácil de
                          estudiar
```

Jugar con el tema. ¿Qué pasó? ¿Sigue su hijo con interés en el tema?

DESCUBRE LO QUE SABE SU HIJO SOBRE EL TEMA.

Las preguntas del hijo ayuda a los padres en ser los guías del proyecto, y también planear las excursiones.

¿Qué sabe mi hijo(a) sobre el tema?

Puede recordar que quiere saber su hijo por:

- Hacer una telaraña
- Hacer una lista de preguntas del hijo(a)
- Guardar los dibujos
- Tomar fotos
- Escribir lo que dice sobre el tema

Haga una lista/ telaraña con su hijo sobre lo que sabe del tema

Haga una lista de preguntas con su hijo sobre el tema, ¿Qué quiere saber el hijo?

Escribe lo que sabe su hijo(a) sobre el proyecto. ¿Cuáles son las ideas, preguntas, y conocimientos que ya tiene?

Teaching Your Child to Love Learning, Copyright © 2004 by Teachers College, Columbia University

COMO HACER PREGUNTAS PARA LA INVESTIGACIÓN

Es importante que los niños busquen respuestas para las preguntas que tienen. Muchas veces nos sorprenden con todo lo que saben. Por ejemplo, puede ser que quieren saber ¿dónde cena el bombero? O ¿qué hace el pescador con su pescado? Porque queremos que ellos piensen, es importante que investiguen lo que quieren saber. De esta manera podemos apoyar el desarrollo de sus curiosidad y su intelectualidad.

Ud. puede ayudar a su hijo a hacer preguntas siguiendo esta sugerencias:

Miren a las ilustraciones de un libro sobre el tema que le interese a su hijo(a):

¿De qué en este dibujo quieres saber más? ¿Qué es _____?

¿Dónde piensas qué _____? ¿Qué es _____?

¿Quién es esta persona? ¿Quieres saber quien hace_____?

¿Qué piensas que hace el _____?

¿Por qué hacen _____?

Además Ud. puede presentar un ejemplo con sus propias preguntas.

Me gustaría saber ¿qué es eso? ¿Para qué podrían usarlo?

Diario para el padre de familia: ¿Cuáles preguntas tiene su hijo(a) sobre el tema?

LA PREPARACIÓN PARA LA INVESTIGACIÓN

Mientras preparas para la investigación, Ud. tendrá muchas cosas para considerar: el ambiente, materiales, y tiempo. Cada uno de este asuntos puede ser fácil con un poco de planificación y organización.

1. ¿Cómo puede proveer un ambiente para apoyar el aprendizaje?
   - ❑ ¿Dónde puedo encontrar el suficiente espacio para trabajar con mi hijo(a)?
   - ❑ ¿Dónde me siento cómoda para trabajar con mi hijo(a)?
   - ❑ ¿Hay un lugar donde mi hijo(a) tiene una superficie para poder escribir, pintar, y trabajar con plastilina?

2. ¿Cómo puedo guardar los materiales y equipo para los proyectos?
   - ❑ ¿Dónde podremos el papel, la plastilina, y los libros sobre el tema del proyecto?
   - ❑ ¿Dónde puedo guardar el proyecto que no han acabado, donde ni el perro o el hijo más chiquito lo va a molestar?
   - ❑ ¿Dónde puedo guardar materiales en un lugar limpio y seguro, pero aún accesible para mi hijo(a)?

3. ¿Cómo puedo encontrar tiempo para hacer proyectos ú otras maneras de aprendizaje?
   - ❑ ¿Hay una hora especial cuando podemos hacer nuestro trabajo del proyecto?
   - ❑ ¿Es posible hacerlo entre el partido de fútbol y el trabajo, o durante la siesta del bebé?

Mientras Ud. prepara los materiales necesarios para los proyectos, las siguientes preguntas le puede ayudar para juntar los materiales básicos y herramientas necesarias.

Preguntas sobre los materiales:
- ¿En qué podemos pintar? (ejemplo: la mesa, el caballete)
- ¿Con qué vamos a pintar? (ejemplo: pinceles, esponjas)
- ¿En qué podemos dibujar? (ejemplo: papel, la pizarra)
- ¿Con qué vamos a dibujar? (ejemplo: marcadores, tiza, crayolas)
- ¿Cómo vamos a pegar? (ejemplo: goma, pegamento)
- ¿Qué podemos usar para cortar? (ejemplo: tijeras de niño, tijeras de adulto)
- ¿Qué podemos usar para moldar? (ejemplo: arcilla, plastilina)
- ¿Cómo vamos a limpiar? (ejemplo: trapos, escobas, toallas)

Segunda Fase

LA INVESTIGACIÓN

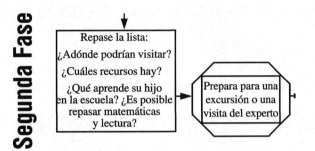

Segunda Fase

Repase la lista:

¿Adónde podrían visitar?

¿Cuáles recursos hay?

¿Qué aprende su hijo en la escuela? ¿Es posible repasar matemáticas y lectura?

Prepara para una excursión o una visita del experto

Diario del padre: La excursión ¿Qué espero que mi hijo(a) aprenda? ¿Cómo lo(a) puedo ayudar a tener una experiencia buena en la excursión?

PREPARACIÓN PARA LA INVESTIGACIÓN

Ya que Ud. entiende más acerca de lo que quiere saber su hijo(a), puede pensar en las maneras de ayudar a su hijo(a) a prepara para la investigación del tema. Unos recursos que le pueden ayudar son:

- ❏ Los libros
- ❏ Plastilina, arcilla, o los bloques Legos
- ❏ Una visitante o amigo quien sabe sobre el tema
- ❏ Los objetos y artículos para explorar

En este momento, piense en unos lugares que podrías visitar con su hijo(a) para investigar este tema. ¿Dónde podrían ir para aprender?

Preparación:
¿Cómo puedo ayudar a mi hijo(a) con su investigación?

- ❏ Discusión
- ❏ Hacer la lista de preguntas
- ❏ Asignar las tareas para la investigación

DESCUBRE NUEVA INFORMACIÓN

Ahora tiene la oportunidad para ayudar a su hijo(a) aprender más sobre el tema y ayudarle(la) a buscar las respuestas de sus preguntas. Pueden visitar a algún sitio, conversar con otras personas, coleccionar unos artículos tangibles, estudiar los libros, o algunas fotos. Provee un evento compartido entre los padres y el hijo(a). Pueden sugerir a su hijo(a) que use sus habilidades de observar, conversar, dibujar, y pintar. Puedes recomendar que su hijo(a) haga las preguntas.

¿Cómo puede preparar su hijo (a) para esta experiencia?

❏ Discutir   ❏ Practicar   ❏ Anotar   ❏ Ensayar

Diario del padre sobre la excursión: ¿Cuál tipo de experiencia quiero que tenga mi hijo(a)? ¿Qué es lo que quiero que descubra mi hijo (a)?

IDENTIFICAR Y ENCONTRAR A LOS EXPERTOS

En el método llamado proyecto, los niños tienen mucha interacción con los adultos (o niños mayores de edad) para encontrar las respuestas a sus preguntas. "Experto" en el trabajo de los proyectos refiere a cualquiera persona quien sepa más que el niño sobre el tema. Es más importante encontrar a un experto que pueda hablar con los niños a un nivel apropiado, que es buscar a un experto bien reconocido. Por ejemplo, Tío Harry quien tiene una camioneta nueva y que le gusta muchas las camionetas puede ser un mejor experto para su niño que un profesor de mecánica.

Definir las destrezas necesarias del experto

¿Cuáles son las destrezas que podrían compartir?
¿Tienen objetos tangibles que podrían prestarle a su hijo (a) para su investigación?
¿Pueden pasar el tiempo libre con su familia?
¿Pueden hacer la actividad? (Por ejemplo, quizás abuelito pueda dar muchos
    consejos sobre los cebos para pescar pero el no puede caminar al riachuelo.)
¿Quiero que mi hijo pase tiempo con esta persona? (A menudo los niños miran
    a los expertos como modelos para imitar.)

Diario del padre: Encontrar a un experto ¿Qué tipo de experto necesitamos? ¿A dónde puedo encontrarlo?

LLEVAR A SU HIJO A LA EXCURSIÓN

¿Necesito transporte para llegar al sitio? ¿Es necesario avisar a los expertos que vamos a venir? ¿Cómo puedo avisarles que estudia mi hijo(a) y lo que queremos saber?

1 o 2 semanas antes de la excursión:

¿Es necesario_____?

❏ Llamar al sitio que visitamos   o   ❏ visitar el sitio antes de que vaya mi hijo (a)

Piense en comunicarse con la persona a quien van a visitar para . . .

- discutir los asuntos de la seguridad
- compartir la importancia de la investigación y las preguntas del hijo(a)
- explicar lo que ya sabe su hijo(a) y lo que ya entiende sobre lo que estudia la importancia de mostrar a su hijo(a) los objetos tangibles, con los que su hijo puede jugar
- explicar como su hijo va a recordar lo que aprende una grabación, video, escritura en un tablero de dibujo, las fotos
- preguntar ¿hay algunas escenas que puede dibujar su hijo(a)?
- preguntar ¿hay algunas herramientas, productos, etc. que nos puede prestar para más investigación?

* Es mejor que deje lo suficiente tiempo para la visita, para que su hijo(a) no se sienta que necesita que tener prisa.

Notas:

En el día de la excursión

Materiales y recursos necesarios:

____ tableros de dibujar
____ equipo de grabar   ❏ una cámara   ❏ video
____ papel, lápices, o crayolas
____ bolsas de plástico o cajas para artefactos que quiera llevar
____ otros

Muchas veces, durante la investigación y la excursión, los niños hacen preguntas nuevas. Puede ser que Ud. necesite provee recursos adicionales para cumplir con esta necesidad nueva.

COMO AYUDAR A SU HIJO A REPRESENTAR SU APRENDIZAJE

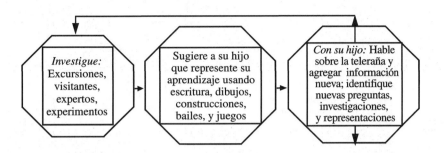

¿Puede repasar mi hijo(a) sus experiencias y trabajo? ¿De cuál manera?

❑ Hablar sobre los dibujos
❑ Dictar la experiencia
❑ Crear un álbum de recortes

❑ o Su primer / segundo dibujos
❑ Revisar la tela de araña
❑ Hacer una exposición

❑ Repasar las fotos
❑ Contestar las preguntas de la listas

¿Cómo puedo introducir a mi hijo recursos nuevos?

❑ Introducir libros nuevos   ❑ Agregar más objetos sobre el tema
❑ Apoyar el juego dramático de mi hijo(a)

¿Podría representar mi hijo(a) su aprendizaje? ¿De cuál manera?

❑ Los dibujos   ❑ Las pinturas   ❑ Las construcciones
❑ El juego   ❑ Cuentos orales

¿De cuál manera podría apoyar a mi hijo(a) en su representación?

¿De cuál manera podría ayudar a mi hijo(a) a desarrollar estas destrezas?

❑ Maneras de resolver ¿Hay un problema que mi hijo podría resolver, el solo?

❑ El desarrollo de las destrezas de pegar, usar cinta, y organizar los materiales

¿Cuáles son las destrezas de la escuela (la lectura, la escritura, la matemática) que podría usar mi niño en este proyecto? (repase el capitulo 5)

¿Hay recursos adicionales que pueda traer a la casa para que su hijo(a) busque más información para que aprenda a un nivel más profundo?

❑ Los libros
❑ Materiales de construcción
❑ Adultos que se puedan entrevistar
❑ Objetos con que su hijo(a) pueda jugar y manipular

Tercera Fase
COMO ACABAR EL PROYECTO

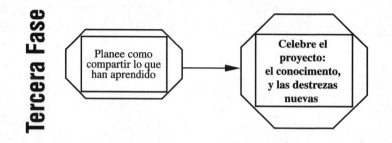

Todos los proyectos tienen un fin. Es un proceso natural. Unos proyectos son más cortos que otros. (Algunos proyectos duran unos meses.) Cuando puede contestar "sí" a estas preguntas, es tiempo de acabar el proyecto.

_____ ¿Está satisfecho(a) su hijo(a)?

_____ ¿Requiere más habilidades de lo que tiene su hijo, para estudiar este tema más? (Por ejemplo: arreglar un carro o manejar)

_____ ¿Ya perdió su niño(a) su interés en el tema?

¿PORQUÉ ES QUE CULMINADOS Y CELEBRAMOS?

Aunque todo los proyectos terminarán, debemos celebrarlos de alguna manera. Haga una mirada detrás, piense en lo que ha aprendido su niño y lo que sucedió en el proyecto para ayudar su hijo(a) con su confianza en si mismo(a). Ayuda a los niños mucho cuando nosotros identificamos lo que significa aprender y los sentimientos de satisfacción que vienen del aprendizaje. La celebración ayuda al niño sentir la terminación del proyecto. También, el proceso de celebrar les dará los recuerdos entrañables en los anos que siguen.

No este sorprendido si se acaba el interés del niño sin terminar el proyecto. Acuérdese que el más importante es que su hijo(a) **piense, investigue, y empiece a considerarse como una persona que pueda aprender.** No es necesario que todos los niños acaben sus proyectos. Los niños exploran muchos intereses antes de encontrar las cosas que a ellos les gustan más. Cuando sí encuentren un proyecto que les guste, puede durar por muchos años y volverse una vocación.

LA EVIDENCIA DEL APRENDIZAJE

Es muy útil tomar el tiempo para hacer una colección de lo que aprendió su hijo y las destrezas que desarrolló. Puede documentar por

- ❏ los dibujos
- ❏ las listas
- ❏ la fotografía
- ❏ las telas de araña
- ❏ las construcciones
- ❏ el juego
- ❏ las pinturas
- ❏ los murales
- ❏ hacer una colección
- ❏ los productos del lenguaje como la escritura, diagramas, cuadros y gráficas

CELEBRAMOS EL PROYECTO

Por lo general, los proyectos culminan en una manera que capta y ayuda a recordar la experiencia. Su hijo(a) puede:

Hacer un modelo
Empezar un álbum de recortes
Enseñar su aprendizaje por el juego dramático (tomen fotos)
Empezar una colección
Pintar
Tomar fotos
Dibujar
Hacer un video
Compartir su proyecto con amigos o parientes
Hacer una presentación del proyecto para su clase en la escuela

Los niños jóvenes no saben hacer estas cosas la primera vez; Ud. tendrá que ayudarlo. A pesar de esto, acuérdese que el niño debe dirigir la celebración del proyecto. Puede ser que el álbum de recortes no salga muy elegante o el modelo no aparezca realista. Sobre todo, es más importante que su hijo(a) haga el trabajo y que se sienta orgulloso de su trabajo.

Diario del padre—culminar el proyecto: ¿Cómo podría Ud. ayudar a su niño a culminar el proyecto y sentir que todos han cumplido sus metas?

EL PRÓXIMO PROYECTO

Diario del padre: ¿Hay otro tema que resultó del proyecto? ¿Es un tema que queremos investigar ahora o en el futuro?

Una última consideración para los padres: ¿Qué aprendió Ud. en hacer este proyecto con su hijo(a)? ¿Qué aprendió Ud. sobre las fortalezas y intereses de su niño? ¿Cómo podría apoyar a su hijo con su aprendizaje en el futuro?